PHILIP RADCLIFFE

MOZART
Piano Concertos

BBC MUSIC GUIDES

ARIEL MUSIC
BBC PUBLICATIONS

Published by BBC Publications
A division of BBC Enterprises Ltd
35 Marylebone High Street, London W1M 4AA

ISBN 0 563 20487 7

First published 1978
Reprinted 1981
First published, with revisions, in Ariel Music 1986

Typeset in 10/11 pt Garamond by Phoenix Photosetting, Chatham
Printed in England by Mackays of Chatham Ltd

Contents

Salzburg 7

Youthful Works (K.37, 39–41, 175) 9

The Concertos of 1776 (K.238, 242, 246) 11

'Jeunehomme' Concerto (K.271) 13

Concerto for Two Pianos (K.365) 16

Vienna 1782–4 19

The Three Concertos of 1782 (K.413–15) 20

The Six Concertos of 1784 (K.449–51, 453, 456, 459) 28

Vienna 1785–91 46

The Three Concertos of 1785 (K.466–7, 482) 46

The Three Concertos of 1786 (K.488, 491, 503) 53

The 'Coronation' Concerto (K.537) 62

Concerto in B flat (K.595) 64

Index of Piano Concertos 68

To Roy Howat

Salzburg

Of all the familiar musical forms, the classical concerto comes nearest to opera. As the eighteenth century proceeded, the solid contrapuntal texture of the baroque era began to seem old-fashioned, and the idea of a single melodic line, standing out against a supporting background, which had been the basis of opera since the beginning of the seventeenth century, began to penetrate into instrumental music. This can be seen in the symphonies of the Mannheim composers, but still more in the concertos, in which the soloist, as it were, frequently takes the stage. And, as Donald Tovey pointed out many years ago, the first movement of the classical concerto, with its introductory orchestral tutti, has much in common with the operatic aria. It is therefore hardly surprising that Mozart, one of the few great composers to whom opera and instrumental music made an equally strong appeal, should have found the concerto a particularly congenial form.

The musical idiom that he had inherited from Johann Christian Bach and other composers of the period was elegant and urbane. On the other hand, his own personality contained a streak of feverish intensity, and it is the combination of these two elements that gives his music its peculiar fascination. He had an unfailing sense of beauty of sound, and there is no reason to suppose that he was consciously concerned with the extension of the musical language of his day. But within the limits of that language he was always alive to the possibilities of contrast, and inevitably this found fullest expression in the marvellous characterisation in his operas. However, it can also be felt in the concertos. The mere fact of his having both a solo instrument and an orchestra made him even more than usually prolific in melodic invention, but when studying Mozart's powers as a melodist it must be remembered that he lived at a time when composers were not in the slightest degree concerned with the deliberate avoidance of clichés. The ultimate character of a theme could easily depend less on the initial melodic idea than its presentation or continuation. For instance, the first four bars of the second section of Leporello's 'catalogue' aria in *Don Giovanni* and of the slow movements of the String Quartet in D Major, K.575, the Quintet for piano and wind, K.452, and the Piano Sonata in C, K.545, are practically identical in melodic outline, but all four passages have their own individual character, and continue on very different lines.

An attempt to distinguish between those of Mozart's themes that are built mainly on conventional formulae and those that are wholly personal in character is an intriguing but treacherous undertaking, if only because of the vast mass of music written by his lesser contemporaries. In general it may be said that Mozart relies most upon formulae in his more ceremonious passages, and is more personal in lyrical moods. But it is not always easy to put one's finger on the personal touch, and individual reactions may differ. Chromaticism often plays an important part: of the four passages mentioned, that from the C major Piano Sonata derives a particularly personal character from the chromaticism in the third bar, and it would be hard to find a more quintessentially Mozartian theme than the exquisite second subject of the first movement of the Piano Concerto in A, K.488. The graceful coloratura of Italian opera permeates the whole of his music. But sometimes, as when writing music for the comic characters in *Die Entführung* and *Die Zauberflöte*, he uses a homelier, more rustic idiom. Sometimes in his instrumental music he amuses himself, and us, by 'dressing up': in the finale of the Violin Concerto in G, K.216, he disguises himself first as a courtier and then as a peasant, and in the finale of the A major Violin Concerto, K.219, he appears in Turkish costume, foreshadowing the finale of the A major Piano Sonata.

The piano concertos contain nothing as unorthodox as this, but there is endless variety of mood and content. In addition to his fertility of invention, Mozart was, in the best sense of the word, a magnificent showman with a sure sense of the most effective moment at which to introduce his ideas. His treatment of form was not as adventurous as that of Haydn, but it was not mechanically conventional. He could be very resourceful in the development of his themes, but there were obviously times when he felt far more inclined to write a new tune than to develop one that already existed, and he had no hesitation in following this urge even if it came at a moment when a well-behaved composer was expected to 'develop'. The dramatist in him probably realised that the unexpected can be particularly telling, especially if it is reserved for special moments and is not overworked. In the longer movements of the piano concertos the exceptional wealth of material gave exceptional opportunities of reintroducing them in an unusual order. This is particularly true of some of the endlessly tuneful and inventive finales, which often achieve a kind of sublime gaiety, but are at the same time highly exhilarating and deeply moving.

Mozart was a pianist from an early age and his writing for the instrument varied considerably. Apart from the Fantasia in C minor, K.475, the Fantasia and Fugue, K.394, and the sombre and passionate Sonatas in A minor, K.310, and C minor, K.457, the solo works are for the most part intimate in mood and spare in texture, though several of the latest sonatas contain contrapuntal writing, sometimes surprisingly harsh in sound. But in the concertos there is far more variety, as can be expected from the more spacious scale on which they are planned. There is nothing as rhetorical as the opening of Beethoven's Piano Concerto in E flat or as swash-buckling as that of the Tchaikovsky Concerto in B flat minor. But the keyboard texture can sometimes be surprisingly rich and sonorous, in a manner far removed from the Victorian conception of Mozart, the charming wonderchild who never wholly grew up. He had more faith in the sustained, singing tone of the keyboard instruments for which he wrote than had Haydn, and he did not hesitate to give them lyrical passages of a touching simplicity, of a kind that would stand out with particular effectiveness against an orchestral background.

Quite early in life Mozart acquired a strong sense of instrumental colour, both in orchestral and in chamber music, and the contrasts that could be obtained between piano and orchestra appealed to him more and more. The early concertos for violin and for flute have great charm, and the much later concerto for clarinet is full of beauty of a gentle and reflective kind. The symphonies and piano sonatas that he wrote in his last years are, in their different ways, of very high quality, but it is clear that in the piano concertos he could combine the features that appealed to him most in the other two media, and the quality of the results reaches so high a general standard that the piano concertos constitute an exceptionally fascinating and lovable part of Mozart's instrumental output.

YOUTHFUL WORKS (K.37, K.39–41 AND K.175)

Mozart showed his interest in piano concertos as early as 1765, when he arranged three of Johann Christian Bach's keyboard sonatas as concertos. Two years later appeared four concertos, K.37, 39, 40 and 41. For many years these were accepted as genuine Mozart, until Wyzeva and Saint-Foix discovered that they were arrangements of sonata movements by Raupart, Honauer, Schobert, Eckard and C. P. E. Bach. Being wise after the event, it is easy to see that they do not show any very individual traits, but they do contain some agreeable music. The Andante of K.37 is the only movement that has not been traced to another source. Eric Blom suggested that it might be Mozart's own work, and a decidedly impressive moment near the end, when the music goes into the tonic minor, seems to bear out this possibility. Although this passage is only a few bars long, it produces a very striking effect in its context, and the sustained note on the horn is a happy orchestral touch, prophetic of later things.

In general, the scoring of these works is simple and unadventurous, but by 1773 when Mozart composed his first original Piano Concerto, in D, K.175, he had written a number of symphonies, all pleasant and fluent, though of no great distinction. The Concerto was written at the end of the year, and was for some time a favourite of its composer. The orchestra consists of two oboes, two horns, two trumpets, drums and strings, and the bustling atmosphere of the first movement suggests that of the overture to a comic opera. The themes are lively and incisive; the only hint of lyricism comes in the short development section, which opens in an unusual manner with a glance at the first subject in the key of the tonic.

The second and third movements are in the same form as the first, a full sonata form preceded by the usual orchestral tutti, announcing the two main themes in the tonic. In the slow movement the development consists of a reflective passage over a dominant pedal, which fore-shadows a very similar procedure that occurs at exactly the same moment in the Andante of the great C major Concerto, K.503. There are other attractive features; the three-bar phrase with which it opens is highly characteristic, especially the first six notes, which almost con-stitute a 'fingerprint':

Ex.1

and there are some pleasant touches of chromaticism and the quietly rocking phrase that ends the opening tutti and the whole movement. The thoughtful mood anticipates many later slow movements.

In the finale Mozart is concerned with a technical problem that obviously fascinated him – the introduction of contrapuntal elements into a movement basically in sonata form. The finale of the String Quar-tet in G, K.387, and the Overture to *Die Zauberflöte* show in what widely different ways the problem can be solved, the one emphasising the contrasts of texture with an exquisitely light touch, and the other fusing them into a rich and solidly built structure. Inevitably, the finale of this early concerto may seem rather naïve by comparison, but the contrast between the boldly canonic opening of the first group and the light-hearted little tunes of the second is most effective. The entry of the soloist is a very happy moment. Realising, no doubt, that the long notes of the main theme would not be suitable for a keyboard instrument, Mozart gives it instead a vivaciously running counterpoint, following the outline of the theme as played by the orchestra. Shortly before the cadenza there is an orchestral passage that gives a momentary glimpse of the finale of the 'Jupiter' Symphony. It is interesting to put this Concerto beside the Symphony in G minor, K.183, which was written at much the same time. In the Concerto the composer is displaying his resources with the energy and enthusiasm to be expected in the first attempt in a particular medium. But in the Symphony, the so-called 'Little G minor', No. 25, the texture is on the whole simpler and the emotional appeal far more direct. These two works, in addition to their prophecies, give a clear indication of the wide range of Mozart's genius.

THE CONCERTOS OF 1776 (K.238, K.242 AND K.246)

The Concerto in B flat, K.238, was written in Salzburg in 1776 and is of a more intimate and lyrical character than its predecessor. There are no trumpets or drums and, very unusually for a concerto, all three movements end quietly. The first movement is more subdued than that of K.175: it is for the most part cheerful and contented, though there is a surprisingly passionate outburst in the development section. But the features that remain most vividly in the memory are the gently syncopated phrase that occurs during the second group, and the lively cadential figure that looks ahead to the first movement of the G major String Quartet, K.387, and rounds off the tutti and the whole movement:

Ex.2

The andante is in a simple sonata form without development. It is an attractive and unusual movement, the subdued colouring of the muted strings, with flutes substituted for oboes, contrasting oddly with the undercurrent of restlessness suggested by the wayward rhythm of the main theme (see Ex. 3 overleaf).

Ex.3

As in the slow movements of some of the later concertos, the atmosphere suggests some kind of serenade. The finale is less sophisticated and more popular in tone than that of K.175. It is in rondo form which, in a piano concerto, usually means that there will be an abundance of tunes. The most striking part is the central episode, which has considerable intensity. The quietly unceremonious conclusion recalls the final bars of the Violin Concertos in G and A, which had been written during the previous year.

The other two concertos of 1776 are less interesting. K.242 in F, for three pianos, was written for the Countess Lodron and her two daughters. The fact that the third piano part is decidedly easier than the others suggests that the second daughter was not a very accomplished pianist, and Mozart made an alternative version for two pianos only. The martial rhythm of the opening theme is a feature that recurs frequently in the piano concertos, but the movement as a whole is diffuse and rather empty. The problem of providing scope for the technique of more than one soloist was solved more satisfactorily by Mozart in the slightly later Concerto for two pianos, K.365, and still more in the great Sinfonia Concertante for violin and viola, K.364, where there is the added interest of the contrasted tone-colour of the two instruments. The *Tempo di Minuetto* finale has something of the same volubility, though the thematic material is more attractive. By far the finest part of the work is the slow movement, the only one among the piano concertos (except for K.488, p. 53) to be marked 'Adagio'. The main theme is richly expressive and contains the fingerprint already mentioned in connection with the slow movement of K.175:

Ex.4

Throughout the movement the chromaticisms and appoggiaturas are very characteristic of Mozart's maturest style and the decorative passages are never mechanical. The return of the first theme, in particular, is beautifully contrived.

The Concerto in C, K.246, contains nothing as fine as this slow movement, but it is a more satisfactory work as a whole. The first movement, like that of K.238, has the unusual direction 'Allegro aperto'. It is lively and energetic, with traces of Mozart's imaginativeness in the handling of the form. One of the most fascinating aspects of Mozart's concertos is the variety of ways with which he first introduces the solo instrument. If, as quite frequently, it enters with the main theme, it is usually over a more animated accompanying figure than before. Here the entry is given special point by the first three notes of the theme being anticipated in the last bar of the opening tutti. The second group contains several themes, of which the most lyrical and attractive does not appear in the tutti but is reserved for the exposition proper. And, conversely, a lively phrase that occurs near the end of the tutti does not reappear until just before the cadenza. The slow movement, like those of K.175 and K.242, is in full sonata form complete with tutti, but is simpler and homelier than either of them. The finale, like that of K.242, is a leisurely rondo in minuet tempo; it is less florid and more varied in content. But neither of these movements makes an entirely satisfactory conclusion to their respective concertos; somehow there is the impression of an attempt to turn the placid grace of the minuet into a brilliance and energy that do not come naturally to it. Some years later Mozart solved the problem with far more success in the most subdued and intimate of his piano concertos, the F major, K.413. Though not in any way a masterpiece, K.246 is an interesting work: Mozart is showing an increased awareness of the infinite variety with which the concerto form can be handled, and there are things in the orchestration, such as the sustained Gs played by the first violin shortly after the entry of the soloist, that are highly characteristic of Mozart in their unobtrusive effectiveness.

'JEUNEHOMME' CONCERTO, K.271 (1777)

With all their attractive features, there is nothing in these early concertos to compare with the extraordinary originality and imaginativeness of K.271, in E flat, written early in 1777 for Mlle Jeunehomme. This can be felt immediately in the opening bars:

13

Ex.5

After this first phrase, the piano enters and obligingly finishes the sentence. Equally original is the re-entry of the soloist after the tutti with a trill, giving the effect of someone who wishes to join in the general conversation without any self-assertion or rhetoric. The tutti itself is concerned largely with the material of the second group, which is of delightfully lyrical quality. The opening theme, which incidentally was recalled in a very different mood in the first movement of the G minor String Quintet, is fully treated here in the development section. In Mozart's piano concertos this section of the first movement, though sometimes very tense, is often mainly devoted to new material. Here, however, the main theme is worked with an almost Beethoven-like insistence. It is only allowed a rest in the final stages of the development in order that it may return more effectively for the recapitulation. At this stage the phrase with which the piano made its first entry undergoes some exciting tonal adventures, and it is also recalled just before the cadenza. Mozart very seldom reintroduces the soloist after the cadenza but in this movement, exceptionally, the final bars of the opening tutti, with the trill for the piano, return with delightful effect just before the concluding flourishes. The whole movement has a remarkable feeling of fresh adventurousness and, as often in the later works, underneath the liveliness and charm there is a strong undercurrent of drama, which is particularly suitable in view of the surprisingly sombre character of what is to follow.

Neither Haydn nor Mozart wrote many slow movements in minor keys, though with both composers they are more frequent in earlier than in later works. But there are more in Mozart's piano concertos than in any other branch of his instrumental works, and they are all of very striking quality. The second movement of K.271 is marked 'andantino', which at that time indicated a slower pace than andante. It has a remarkable intensity, which shows itself in various ways. In some ways it is very operatic, with passages for the soloist that come near to recitative, and from time to time a cadential figure that was a common formality in the opera of the period, but here (Ex. 6) has a strangely grim and menacing effect. But at the same time it must be remembered that counterpoint, though not the all-pervading element that it had been

Ex.6

during the baroque period, still had its part to play in the latter half of the eighteenth century. When the minor composers of the day wrote fugally, the result, however efficient, was liable to sound like imitation Handel. But for composers of the calibre of Mozart and Haydn counterpoint could still be felt as something vital and exciting, and Mozart's fugal writing is sometimes startlingly hectic and uncompromising. In the slow movement of K.271 there is nothing that can be described as fugal, but its intensity is due not only to its operatic quality but to its subtlety of texture. In the sombre opening bars the first and second violins play in canon, and shortly afterwards this passage is repeated under a new and more florid melody played by the soloist, producing some surprisingly harsh clashes. The form of the movement resembles that of K.238, being in sonata form without development; it opens with a short tutti which as usual anticipates features of both the first and second group. As in the first movement, the second group is spacious and eventful; its very appealing first phrase is curiously like one that occurs in the slow movement of J. S. Bach's Violin Concerto in E major.

In any concerto movement in sonata form the opening of the recapitulation is an interesting moment. It usually consists of some kind of telescoping of the opening tutti and the exposition of the first movement, and often, as in K.175 and K.238, the first theme on its return is neatly shared by piano and orchestra. In this movement the piano plays the first two bars of the main theme and then continues with the more ornate melody of its original entry. Very surprisingly, the second group opens as before in the relative major but soon moves to C minor. As so often in Mozart, the recalling in the minor key of what had previously been heard in the major produces a peculiarly pathetic and nostalgic effect. After the cadenza the movement ends with a few bars of dialogue between the piano and orchestra, the two final chords, unusually for a slow movement, being marked '*forte*'. Two years later, in the Sinfonia Concertante for violin and viola, K.364, Mozart wrote a slow movement, also in C minor, which has much the same poignancy as that of K.271.

The finale of this concerto is as exuberant as the andantino is sombre. Although a rondo, it does not display the immense wealth and variety of melodic invention that is usually to be found when Mozart uses this form. Apart from the very surprising central episode, the general impression is of an irrepressible rush of energy with a few subsidiary ideas, but all stemming ultimately from the main theme. This, as Professor Hutchings has pointed out,[1] anticipates Monostatos in Act 2 of *Die Zauberflöte*, but it also has a touch of Beethoven in the sense of firm control that can be felt behind the constant flow of rapid notes. On its final appearance it is played by the first oboe, against a background of pizzicato strings, the piano playing above it a long trill reminiscent of its first entry in the first movement. The juxtaposition of *pianissimo* and *forte* in the final bars again looks forward to Beethoven. But the most unusual feature of this movement is the central episode, which almost amounts to a separate movement. It is a minuet with two leisurely strains, both of which are played twice, first by the piano alone and then in a gracefully varied form against a picturesquely scored orchestral background. It is not only very attractive in itself, but particularly effective owing to the lack of sustained melodic material in the rest of the finale. And here there is no feeling, as in K.242 and K.246, that the gentle measure of the minuet is being pushed into rather uncongenial channels. The passage that leads back to the main tempo is one of the most luxuriant that Mozart ever wrote, the piano playing full arpeggios against a simple but very rich background. The whole work is an important landmark in Mozart's output of concertos; it has something of the freshness and adventurousness of some of the slightly earlier violin concertos, but is larger in scope and more varied in mood. Mozart wrote cadenzas for all three movements; the work's most unusual feature, the introduction of a slower episode into the finale, was reproduced many years later in another Concerto in the same key, K.482, which suggests that K.271 may have held a rather special place in his affections.

CONCERTO FOR TWO PIANOS (K.365)

Two years later, in 1779, Mozart wrote the Concerto in E flat for two pianos, K.365, for himself and his sister Nannerl. This is a less imaginative, perhaps more conventional work than K.271, but it is far more successful than the Concerto for three pianos, and is far from being merely a showpiece. It would be idle to expect in this work the elaborate polyphony of a two-keyboard concerto by J. S. Bach, but the interest is

1   Arthur Hutchings, *A Companion to Mozart's Piano Concertos* (Oxford, 1947).

very skilfully divided between the two soloists, with much graceful and lively conversation. The first movement contains some interesting and unusual points of structure which illustrate well the flexibility with which Mozart could handle the concerto form. The opening tutti is vigorous and eventful. Apart from a few bars towards the end it contains no reference to any part of the second group, but there are several ideas that do not recur until the development section. The second group, as usual, contains a wealth of material, including a pleasant tune which looks ahead to a very similar phrase in the much later D major Concerto, K.537:

Ex.7

The development, again, is unexpected. Opening with a little phrase from the tutti, it soon plunges into a stormy passage which, as so often in the concertos, has no thematic connection with anything else. The music touches briefly on a few extraneous keys, but is soon back in the tonic. An attractive lyrical phrase seems to float in from nowhere and soon disappears, though Mozart alludes to it in his cadenza. A massive build-up on the dominant seventh leads to the reappearance, not of the main theme as would be expected, but of a striking phrase from the tutti, and when the first theme finally returns, it soon wanders into E flat minor, as though to compensate for the lack of tonal adventure in the development. The later stages of the recapitulation are also decidedly free. Both in its massive spaciousness and its structural boldness, this movement foreshadows that of the Sinfonia Concertante for violin and viola, K.364.

The slow movement has none of the emotional depth of that of K.271, but it is a delicate and attractive piece of music. There is less sustained singing melody than in most of Mozart's slow movements, and the conversational element is very pronounced; the first four bars of the main theme were obviously conceived as a dialogue between first violins and oboe in the tutti and subsequently between the two pianos. Under a wealth of elegant and elaborate detail the form of the movement is a very simple ABA design, and the music never settles for more than a short time in any extraneous key. The part played by the orchestra is unobtrusive, but full of exquisite touches; the few bars before the return of the main theme are beautifully coloured, the two final bars of the movement make a peculiarly touching farewell, and the bar before the first entry of the pianos is in its own quiet way decidedly bold.

Ex.8

Though not one of the most immediately appealing of Mozart's slow movements, it has considerably more warmth than its elegant exterior might at first suggest and it contains phrases that remain in the memory in a strangely persistent way.

But the most striking part of this work is the very lively and energetic finale, which at once sweeps aside the courtly manners of the andante. It is a spaciously planned sonata-rondo with a main theme that has great rhythmic drive and is liable to indulge in interrupted cadences at unexpected moments. It is followed at once by another theme still in the tonic that, rather surprisingly, does not recur, though the triplets by which it is accompanied play an important part as the movement proceeds. The theme of the first episode has a vigorous march rhythm, which can be felt in a more subdued manner in the second episode, in C minor. As usual with Mozart, the returns of the main theme are beautifully devised, especially after the C minor episode, when it floats back in a delightfully casual way. Before the recapitulation of the first episode the main theme appears in a more lyrical vein and eventually goes through a chromatic sequence which contrasts vividly with its cheerfully matter-of-fact surroundings. The work as a whole does not quite aspire to the grandeur of the slightly later[1] Sinfonia Concertante for violin and viola, or the emotional power of one or two earlier works, such as the Piano Sonata in A minor, K.310, or the Violin Sonata in E minor, K.304, but its freshness and high spirits make it a very enjoyable work.

1 The Köchel numbers of these works are misleading.

Vienna 1782–4

The Concerto in E flat for two pianos, K.365, is the last piano concerto that Mozart wrote before leaving Salzburg and at this stage it is worth looking back for a moment at the music that he had written up to this point. His instrumental output includes over thirty symphonies, twenty-six violin sonatas, thirteen string quartets, thirteen piano sonatas and only six piano concertos. And, of course, side by side with these, many operatic and other vocal works. Inevitably it is of uneven quality, with much that does little more than talk pleasantly in the idiom of the day without much individuality. But there are a fair number of peaks, of which the Concerto, K.271, is certainly one. But even so it is surprising that at this stage he showed so little interest in the medium that meant so much to him in later years. His next work for piano and orchestra was written in 1782, by which time many things had happened. In 1780 he left Salzburg for Munich, where *Idomeneo* received its first performance; in 1781, he settled at Vienna, where an opera of totally different character, *Die Entführung*, was composed and performed. *Idomeneo* was undoubtedly the longest and finest opera that he had yet written; its grandeur and emotional depth make it a particularly important landmark in his output. It is at least possible that the composition of this intensely powerful and expansive work for the stage may have done much to stimulate Mozart's interest in the most operatic of instrumental forms. It came gradually, however, the first manifestation being the Rondo in D, K.382, written as a substitute for the finale of K.175. Despite its title this is really a set of variations, and it must have been composed as a concession to popular taste, as, although pleasant enough in a rather superficial way, it is nothing like as interesting as the original finale. But the seventeen piano concertos that follow reach an extraordinarily high level; they give a very complete expression of the various sides of Mozart's genius and there are several comparatively unfamiliar ones that, even if not on the very highest level, contain some beautiful and characteristic music. It has already been suggested that counterpoint was for Mozart something far more than an academic ingenuity. He realised, as Handel had done before him, that it can be supremely effective as a means of producing dramatic tension. The magnificent quartet in the third act of *Idomeneo* is the earliest instance of this in the operas, and from this time onward unobtrusive polyphonic effects are liable to appear with seemingly effortless ease in works of any kind. The fugal finale of the early String Quartet in D minor, K.173, is extremely ingenious and effective, but it seems self-conscious compared with the finale of the Quartet in G, K.387, or indeed with the texture of anything in the later chamber music.

THE THREE CONCERTOS OF 1782 (K.413–15)

The next three piano concertos were written in 1782, just before the composition of the six string quartets dedicated to Haydn; it is perhaps significant that they are concise and unassuming works, two of which have something of the intimate character of chamber music. This is particularly true of K.413, in F, a work of much beauty, that has been generally underrated. It is on the whole gentle and unobtrusive but, in the words of Tovey, 'its quiet sagacity is no sign of weakness'. The opening is unexpected; an energetic start leads to a simple, half playful tune; after some more vigorous music, the main theme of the second group enters temporarily in the dominant, a most unusual feature for the opening tutti; this proves to be a subtlety that is explained during the exposition. The entry of the piano is beautifully timed across a cadence, and leads not to the first theme, but to this:

Ex.9

The theme is built on the phrase sometimes known as the 'Mannheim sigh', which eventually became a familiar Mozart fingerprint. The orchestra soon enters with the first subject and the exposition proceeds regularly. The second group enters in the dominant and appears for a moment to be about to return to the tonic as in the tutti. This time, however, it proves to be a feint. As might be expected from the generally lyrical character of the main themes, the development is largely non-thematic, though there is at one point a reference to a passage that preceded the opening of the second group. The recapitulation opens with the graceful passage with which the piano first entered, leading, as before, to the first subject. It then proceeds regularly till the coda. This opens with a vigorous passage that has not been heard since the opening tutti; it leads very effectively to the pause for the cadenza. For this there is a remarkable specimen published in facsimile by Mandycewski; it is in Leopold Mozart's handwriting and, considering the general character of the movement, is surprisingly stormy. Shortly before the end of the movement there is a very happy reference to the passage which, in its previous appearances, led to the phrase with which the soloist first entered. Here, however, it is cut off abruptly by two chords. In several ways the Piano Sonata in F, K.332, written in 1778, provides some interesting parallels with this concerto. The first movements of both works are in triple time, with flowing and melodious themes. The sonata movement is on the whole the more emotional; there is some decidedly sombre and agitated music in both the transition and the development section. In the concerto the general atmosphere is more serene but, as might be expected, the texture is more subtle and the phraseology more varied.

The slow movements of the two works show similar likenesses and differences. Both are in B flat and in slow common time, adagio in the sonata and larghetto in the concerto. The sonata movement, after an elegant opening, goes quietly into the tonic minor at a surprisingly early stage in the movement with an almost Schubertian effect, and there is a restless undercurrent throughout. The slow movement of K.413 is more placid in mood, but also more subtle. Both movements are in a simple sonata form without development, but in the concerto there is a very attractive passage that leads back to the recapitulation, and is recalled shortly before the cadenza. The phraseology of the main theme is noteworthy. Phrases of three or five bars occur from time to time in Mozart's music, though they are more characteristic of Haydn and Schubert. But in the larghetto of K.413 he opens with:

Ex.10

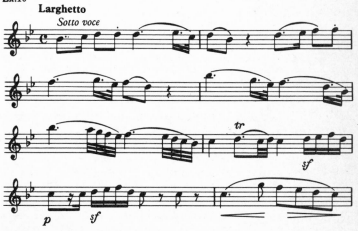

This consists of the familiar eight bars, though it is cunningly disguised by a variety of subdivisions. The opening symphony of 'He was despised' from Handel's *Messiah* has something of the same subtlety. The slow movements of Mozart's piano concertos show considerable variety, both of form and mood. A full sonata form, with or without tutti, is not common in the later works, though when it does appear the results are particularly fine. When, as in this movement, there is no development section, the music tends to be of an idyllic, serenade-like character. Perhaps the loveliest instance is the Allegretto in the F major Concerto, K.459. But the slow movement of K.413, though gentle, is surely no less haunting; its attractions grow with acquaintance.

The third movements of K.332 and K.413 both end quietly but there the resemblance ends. The finale of the sonata is a vigorous and restless movement, covering a considerable variety of mood, while that of the concerto is predominantly lyrical. For the last time in the piano concertos Mozart returns to the moderate minuet tempo, and with far more success than in either of the other instances. For one thing the main theme

Ex.11

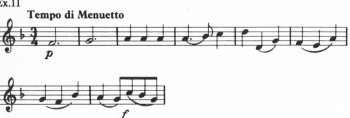

is certainly more distinctive and less conventional than those of the earlier finales; also the texture is full of unobtrusively resourceful part-writing. This provides a pleasant contrast to the slow movement, which consists largely of cantabile melody accompanied simply, though not mechanically, by the alberti bass. The melody of the minuet is never varied, but is presented against a great diversity of background on its reappearances; this is particularly desirable as it is by far the most important melodic idea in the movement. It is in sonata rondo form, but the landmarks are not underlined; there is a very telling stroke when the passage in C major that constitutes the first episode is recapitulated in F minor. Mozart obviously felt that for so intimate a movement a cadenza would be out of place. During its last appearance the main theme seems to grow weary and the end is quiet and delicate. It is very unusual for a work to have first and last movements in 3/4 time, and the finale of this concerto must surely be taken at a decidedly slower pace than the first movement. But the whole work makes a singularly satisfying whole, its modest dimensions being well suited to its quiet demeanour. In its own way this concerto is one of Mozart's most perfect works.

The Concerto in A, K.414, is also an intimate work, the orchestra consisting only of strings, two oboes and horns. Mozart even dispenses with bassoons, which he had used in K.365 and for the slow movement of K.413. But it is full of very attractive themes, and is the best known and most frequently performed of the three piano concertos of 1782. The delightfully genial opening theme:

Ex.12

is very characteristic and must have made a strong appeal to Schubert in his early years, as reminiscences of it can be found in the opening of the slow movement of his first symphony, the second theme of the first movement of his second symphony, and a theme in the first movement of his Piano Sonata in A minor, D.537.

When Mozart opens a concerto, or, indeed, any large work with so frankly melodious a theme, he will probably, with his vivid sense of contrast, follow it with a vigorous passage of a more rhythmic character, and this happens here. Eventually the main theme of the second group appears in the key of the tonic. It has an amiably jaunty and nonchalant air, but it soon gives way to two ideas, neither of which recur till the coda. One is an exciting contrapuntal dialogue that rises with increasing tension over a pedal note, and the other a pleasantly flowing tune; the tutti ends with some lively flourishes. The soloist enters with the main theme and proceeds in a leisurely way to the dominant in a passage built on a transitional theme that grows out of the penultimate bar of the tutti. The first theme of the second group is now shared between orchestra and piano, and it is allowed to expand at greater length than before. By the end of the exposition Mozart has already produced at least four themes, but he is in so insatiably inventive a mood that most of the development section is devoted to yet another tune. Eventually this gives place to some impressive passage work, but there is no reference to any of the previous themes. At the beginning of the recapitulation the piano shares the main theme with the orchestra. In its early stages this recapitulation follows the exposition quite closely, until the return, first of the flowing tune that appeared towards the end of the tutti, and then of the contrapuntal dialogue, which now leads to the cadenza. Finally the movement ends with the flourishes that rounded off the tutti.

The andante is more solidly built than the larghetto of K.413; it is in the same form as the first movement, although it is on a smaller scale. The tutti gives a very concise summary of the themes of the movement; the first has a foretaste of Beethoven in its quiet solemnity and the second (Ex. 13) has a strong similarity to the first theme of the first movement.

Ex.13

Finally there is a gently rocking phrase that plays an unexpectedly important part later on. In the exposition everything has more time to expand, with some richly expressive music for the piano. The development section is far more thematically relevant than that of the first movement, and is built entirely on the rocking phrase with which the exposition ended. The music goes through a number of keys with gradually increasing tension, arriving at an impressive climax before the recapitulation. This is generally regular, although the passages for the piano are rather more subdued than in the exposition. This may be due to the limited range of the keyboard, or to the imminence of the cadenza. Shortly after this, the movement ends, quietly and appropriately, with the rocking phrase. It is interesting to compare this andante with that of the early Concerto in D, K.175. The two are very similar in form and in mood, and the earlier movement contains much that is prophetic. But we can also see how between 1773 and 1782 Mozart's style, though it has not basically changed, has become richer and subtler in every way. The colouring is warmer and more varied and the decorative passages have more intensity. In both movements the part played by the orchestra is unobtrusive, but in the development section of the later movement, the oboes and horns are used more imaginatively.

The finale of K.414 is in a lighter vein than either of the other movements, but its construction is more adventurous and unexpected. It is a sonata rondo and, as in the first movement, there are many themes. Two appear in rapid succession; the first is the livelier, but the second, smooth and sinuous, plays the more important part and is used extensively in the first episode with a variety of harmonic backgrounds. The piano enters, not as might be expected with the main theme, but with a new melody reminiscent of a passage from the finale of the Piano Sonata in C, K.330. After the first episode the main theme returns as usual, after which the sinuous theme leads very effectively to the central episode which introduces a fourth theme. From this point unexpected things happen. The new tune is followed, not by the main theme, but by a recapitulation of the first episode in the tonic. Even after this the first theme does not appear, but instead there is a remarkably exciting passage with the second violins playing a tremolo in demisemiquavers, which leads to the cadenza. Still the first theme refuses to appear, and instead, after the cadenza, the piano recalls the melody with which it made its original entry. It is, however, broken up by unexpected pauses and for one bar the music plunges on to the chord of B flat. But order is soon restored: the first theme makes its long expected reappearance and the movement ends in a brisk and matter-of-fact way, much as the opening tutti had done.

The concerto as a whole is an extremely attractive work, full of the genial friendliness characteristic of Mozart's works in A. In many ways it is a worthy precursor to K.488, though it does not aspire to the mellow richness of the first movement or the poignancy of the second movement of the later work. But it is remarkably successful in its own right and, despite the great merits of K.413 and K.415, it is not surprising that the A major Concerto has achieved wider popularity than either of the others. A rondo for piano and orchestra, K.386, was written at about the same time as K.414, and may at one stage have been intended for its last movement. It is pleasant and flowing, with an attractively wistful second theme, but it has not the sparkle and the adventurousness of K.414 and it would not be surprising to learn that Mozart was not satisfied with it. On the other hand, the fact that he wrote cadenzas for all three movements of K.414 suggests that it may have been a special favourite.

The Concerto in C, K.415, uses an orchestra larger than any that had appeared in previous piano concertos; it contains oboes, horns, bassoons, trumpets and drums. The first movement is full of ideas but, most unusually for Mozart, they seem to be slightly at odds with each other, and unable to make an entirely convincing whole. The opening tutti is spacious and exhilarating; it opens stealthily in a march-like rhythm that looks back to the Concerto for three pianos and ahead to several later concertos. Other ideas follow, including a beautiful sequential passage over a dominant pedal which much resembles a theme in the first movement of the Haffner Symphony of the same year. But, however splendid in itself, this tutti, as Professor Girdlestone has pointed out, [1] contains a surprising amount of music that never returns, and after its very emphatic conclusion, followed by a pause, the entry of the soloist with new material seems almost an anticlimax. The first theme returns for a few bars but, for so incisive a phrase, it plays a surprisingly small part in the movement, and is never given to the piano. The second group contains a pleasant lyrical tune and some lively contrapuntal writing for the soloist, and ends with a reminiscence of the end of the tutti. The development section is concerned largely with new material, but there is a beautiful but all too short passage built round the main theme, and a period of attractively prolonged suspense before the recapitulation. This opens with the soloist's original entry, which is more effective here than in its former context. There are no new features to come; Mozart wrote a cadenza which is very vigorous and effective, but contains no reference to the first theme. In some ways this movement foreshadows that of K.503, also in C major, and the first theme of its second group is very similar to the corresponding feature of the later movement.

Ex.14

But in the first movement of K.503 the many contrasting elements make an extraordinarily convincing structure, whereas in K.415, we sometimes have the impression of a potential symphony into which a part for piano solo has strayed.

Apparently Mozart was at this point uncertain how to continue and the beginning of a slow movement in C minor was abandoned. Instead he wrote a quietly flowing andante in a simple ABA form. It provides an effective contrast to the rather restless outer movements, and there are some charming touches in the orchestral writing, such as the interweaving of the second violin and viola parts at the opening and the high Gs played by the first violins at the beginning of the central episode. But it seems as a whole rather monotonous compared with some of Mozart's

1 Cuthbert Girdlestone, *Mozart et ses concerts pour piano* (Paris, 1939), English translation (1948).

later slow movements. For instance the andante of the Piano Sonata, K.545, uses the alberti bass with even more persistence, but there is enough contrast of key to give it greater vitality, and in the simpler of the concerto slow movements there is more variety of material. Mozart himself may have felt this movement to be over-placid, as he wrote a cadenza for it that has some striking, almost dramatic moments; in performance it could well provide an element of tension lacking in the rest of the movement.

But the most completely successful part of this Concerto is undoubtedly the finale, which is one of Mozart's most original. It is basically a sonata rondo, but with surprising events. The main theme is announced by the piano and repeated by the orchestra, who proceed with a leisurely tutti. This includes the second main theme, which opens with a very attractive five-bar phrase:

Ex.15

When this is finished the tempo changes from 6/8 to 2/4 and the soloist breaks into a melancholy operatic aria in C minor, against a simple but very telling orchestral background. Eventually this ends on a half-close; the first theme returns and proceeds to the first episode, which is based on the second theme. The central episode consists of a strenuous development of the first phrase of the main theme. The first episode is then recapitulated (Ex.15), at one point taking a very unexpected harmonic turn. The C minor passage returns in a more florid form, against a pizzicato accompaniment which intensifies its operatic character. After a final appearance of the first theme the movement ends with what is perhaps the most poetical passage in the work. It is built on the rhythm of the first bar, and the music dies away against a background of murmuring strings and, finally, a *pianissimo* drum-roll. There is nothing quite like this in any other finale by Mozart. The picturesquely contrasted episodes in the finales of the violin concertos have an air of gay inconsequence, with Mozart deliberately appearing in unexpected costumes. The slow interludes in those of K.271 and K.482 have almost the air of separate movements contrasting beautifully with their lively surroundings. But there is something stranger and more mysterious about the C minor passages in the finale of K.415; they cast an unaccountable shadow over the movement, and Mozart may well have felt that after them the usual loud conclusion would have seemed hollow.

The three Concertos, K.413, K.414 and K.415, form an interestingly contrasted group. The most often played, the A major, is also the most completely satisfying, and well deserves its popularity. The F major, with its intimate atmosphere, foreshadows the six string quartets dedicated to Haydn which Mozart was shortly to write. It comes nearest perhaps to K.464 in A major, which also has a first movement in triple time, and a minuet with something of the subtly woven texture of the finale of the Concerto. K.415 is the most unequal of the three, but it is a work of great interest, with one of Mozart's most fascinating finales. These concertos do not aspire to the spaciousness of the later ones, or of the symphonies, but in the first movement of K.415, with its curiously mixed body of thematic ideas, there is a certain feeling of constriction, as though they needed more room for expansion of the kind that gives the first movement of K.503 its greatness. It was two years before the next piano concertos were written and by that time Mozart had written all his symphonies except the last four, and all his piano sonatas except the last five.

THE SIX CONCERTOS OF 1784
(K.449–51, K.453, K.456 AND K.459)

The six piano concertos written in 1784 include three that are widely and deservedly popular and three that have been on the whole underrated. K. 449, in E flat, belongs to the latter category, but it is a fascinating and very individual work. It is not particularly long and requires a small orchestra, with oboes, horns and strings, but it has a curious inner intensity, especially in the first two movements. The opening theme has a tonal ambiguity as a result of which the work is described in the index of the complete Breitkopf and Härtel as being in C minor.

Ex.16

By a curious coincidence it is a melodic inversion of the opening theme of the C minor Concerto, K.491. The tutti is unusually restless; soon there is an agitated theme in C minor that does not reappear till near the end, and one of the themes of the second group appears in the dominant. There are other ideas, and the rhythm of the third bar of the first theme plays an important part. The theme itself is given in a varied form to the piano for its first entry. The second group is attractively varied in mood. An elegantly flowing melody leads to the very characteristic theme that has already appeared in the tutti. This is followed by some lively passage work, and finally the exposition ends with reminiscences of the tutti. The development section is fairly short and the first part of it is dominated by the menacing rhythm of bar 3 of Ex. 16. Eventually, however, there is a very impressive lull; the harmonic movement becomes slower and there is a mysterious chromatic passage from which the first theme suddenly emerges for the reprise as though from a tunnel.

A rather similar process occurs at exactly the same moment in the first movement of the E flat Symphony, K.543. There the effect is quietly casual, as of an inspired last-minute impulse; here it is more dramatic. The recapitulation is regular except for a striking interrupted cadence under a trill, which leads to a very effective reminiscence of the C minor theme that had not been heard since the tutti. Similarly, Mozart's cadenza does not refer to the main theme, but recalls an energetic phrase that had appeared in the opening tutti and in the exposition, but not again. Here, as so often, we can see Mozart's skill in deciding on the best moment at which to introduce his ideas, and the special opportunities for this that he must have found in the concerto form.

The andantino that follows is a movement of peculiar intimacy, with a richness of texture and a wide range of modulation that look ahead to Schubert. Its form is not easy to define; it might be described as a cross between sonata and rondo. The leisurely and very expressive main theme is played first by the orchestra and then by the piano, leading eventually to a rather more florid second theme in F major, the dominant. This soon moves to the unexpectedly remote key of A flat, where a shortened version of the first theme is divided between piano and orchestra. The music then moves to E flat, where the second subject reappears, but it is soon plunged into a highly emotional passage which leads by a very devious way to the tonic.

Ex.17

There is then a recapitulation of the two main themes, both in B flat; the second is now played not by the piano, as before, but by the orchestra. Finally there is a coda built on phrases from the first theme that had not appeared since its original presentation, but had been cunningly kept in reserve for the final stages. Commentators have reacted to this movement in oddly diverse ways. Professor Girdlestone[1] describes it as 'calm and guileless' and Einstein[2] referred to its avoidance of pathos and sentimentality. But, to one musician at least, Blom's reference[3] to its 'troubled beauty' seems far nearer the mark. Beneath its polished exterior there is a decided undercurrent of restlessness that fits well with the wayward and independent character of the first movement. It has a striking continuity, with fewer formal cadences than usual and this tendency to avoid emphasis on the familiar landmarks of the form is strongly prophetic of the nineteenth-century music.

The finale is one of Mozart's most original and, like a number of other movements, it shows his extraordinary resourcefulness in the handling of the rondo form. At its earliest stages this was the most sectional of forms; here the landmarks are covered over as skillfully as in the andantino and it is as highly organised as the first movement. It opens with a tutti in which the two main themes are announced. The first has a very distinctive melodic line; the second, which reappeared some years later in the finale of the Piano Sonata in D, K.576, is gentler in character and is never allowed to assert itself for long. The piano enters with the first theme, which is soon accompanied by a very lively variation of itself. The first episode begins with the second theme in the dominant, but soon the first two bars of the first theme appear and seem to be on the point of breaking into a fugue. For the moment, however, this is swept aside by some brilliant writing for the piano. But towards the end of the episode an unexpectedly quiet bar in syncopated rhythm is heard several times; this foreshadows a strange and mysterious passage that is to come

1 Girdlestone, *op. cit.*
2 Alfred Einstein, *Mozart, his character and his work* (New York and Oxford, 1945).
3 Eric Blom, *Mozart* (London, 1935).

later. The first theme returns in due course, this time accompanied by another variation. The second episode opens with an aggressive theme in C minor which might have been in Beethoven's head when he wrote the coda of the rondo of the *Pathétique* Sonata. Soon, however, the irrepressible opening of the first theme appears, also in C minor, and this time the fugal texture continues with great animation, the piano playing lively running passages in quavers that contrast vividly with the spiky outline of the theme.

Eventually the counterpoint gives way to a very impressive passage of prolonged suspense before the next return of the first theme. This is now played in broken octaves by the piano against the original form in the orchestra. The opening phrase of the second episode now appears in the tonic, and leads to a recalling of various elements of the first episode. This, however, does not include the second main theme, which appears for the moment to have been forgotten. But the mysterious syncopated bar casts a far more sombre shadow over the music than before, and for a moment we are in the very remote key of D flat minor. After this Mozart, having already shown immense resourcefulness in varying his theme, now springs a fresh surprise by producing both first and second themes in 6/8 time, much as Beethoven was to do in the finale of his Piano Concerto in C minor. Having done this there is little more to be said and a few bars of charming and slightly nostalgic dialogue between piano and orchestra bring the work to an end. The lively contrapuntal writing looks back to the finale of K.175, but, as might be expected, it is here far more closely integrated into the texture. Never again did Mozart use so small an orchestra for a concerto; even the wind parts here can be dispensed with. But in content and imagination it is a remarkably fine work that deserves to be far more often performed.

The Concerto in B flat, K.450, is a work of very different character. The piano part is more brilliant and exacting, the texture, despite the larger orchestra, less intricate and the general manner more urbane. This can be felt at once in the cheerful conversation between the wind and the strings with which the work opens. It is followed in the tutti by a number of ideas; a ceremonious passage, a melody of great beauty and simplicity.

Ex.18

This appears first in a very bare texture and is then repeated with a flowing counterpoint, and then comes a lively crescendo of the kind frequently to be found in the symphonies of the Mannheim composers. Finally a neat and playful cadential phrase ends the tutti and the piano enters with an elegant flourish over some detached chords. It then settles down to the first theme and the exposition proceeds. As so often, there are surprises. Ex. 18, which seems ideally fitted to be the main theme of the second group, does not appear, and instead there is a more florid melody. Soon passages from the tutti appear, and the cadential phrase is neatly transformed into a running chromatic figure for the piano. This dominates the first part of the development section but eventually, as in K.449, the music becomes non-thematic and the harmonic movement is impressively broad and deliberate. But the actual returns of the first themes of the two movements are very dissimilar. That of K.449, as we have seen, emerges suddenly after a mysterious chromatic passage; here it is elaborately prepared, first under and then over a trill. The most striking moment in the recapitulation is the return of Ex. 18, more fully accompanied than before. The exciting Mannheim-like crescendo from the tutti leads to the cadenza. Mozart's own cadenza is, as usual, very concise; it does not use the first theme but has a very beautiful reference to Ex. 18. In the final bars there is a reminiscence of the detached chords over which the piano made its original entry, but, as in a similar passage at the end of the first movement of K.413, there is no piano, and they are brushed abruptly aside.

Mention has already been made of the stimulus to Mozart's thematic invention by the presence of both a solo instrument and an orchestra. It was equally stimulating to his resourcefulness in handling the variation form. Apart from the comparatively trivial Rondo, K.382, the slow movement of K.450 is the first appearance of this form in a concerto. It is more unified in mood than the three later sets, but there is no note-for-note repetition. Even the two strains of the theme are played by the strings and then repeated in a slightly varied form by the piano. In the two variations that follow, the repeats of both strains are similarly varied, so that they really amount to four. The movement ends with a short and delicate coda. Despite an appearance on paper of complexity, the variations follow the outline of the theme very closely, though there are occasional unexpected touches in the harmony. The increasingly elaborate figuration in the piano part does little to disturb the quietly contemplative character of the music, and above all it is the touching and intimate beauty of the theme itself that gives the movement its character. The use of pizzicato against the sustained writing for the wind and the florid arpeggios for the piano is a striking and picturesque effect, and the luxuriant richness of the music looks ahead to some of Beethoven's slow movements, especially the Largo of the Piano Concerto in C minor.

Hitherto the wind section in this Concerto has consisted of oboes, horns and bassoons; the addition of a flute for the finale is a very effective touch, very well suited to the lively character of the movement. The first of the three 6/8 time finales in B flat, it has not quite the adventurousness of that of K.456, or the delicacy of that of K.595, but is full of attractive high-spirits. Like most of Mozart's rondos, it has many themes, two of which seem to be strongly connected with the development of keyboard virtuosity. In the first episode there is a chromatic, creeping theme that involves some difficult crossing of hands. In the second episode there is another theme, more extrovert in character, that uses the same device less subtly. There are also some lively hunting calls reminiscent of the horn concertos of the previous year. But the most striking feature of the movement is the very resourceful treatment of the main theme:

Ex.19

This has a catchy and insistent rhythm that could become irritating if overworked, but in Mozart's hands there is no danger of this. In the fourth bar the A flat in the harmony is a charming and characteristic touch; on the theme's reappearance after the first episode and on all subsequent occasions, the quaver F at the end of bar 2 is sharpened. The first phrase dominates the latter part of the second episode. Starting in E flat over repeated chords it touches on a number of keys and then breaks into a contrapuntal argument with a rushing demisemiquaver passage. This gradually subsides; the repeated chords return and from the dominant of D minor the music returns quietly, 'unresting, unhasting', to B flat. The whole passage is beautifully graded; the little two-bar phrase is treated with a persistence prophetic of Beethoven, but with an essentially Mozartian lightness of touch. It also comes nearer to the conventional idea of 'development' than anything in the first movement.

Towards the end of the finale the hunting call is prominent. It becomes the basis of a passage of ten bars built entirely of the chord of B flat which would certainly be taken for a rousing crescendo, were it not for the fact that Mozart directs it to be played *pianissimo*, reserving a *forte* for a final surprise. It is not surprising that this concerto has always been popular; it does not touch on the darker and stranger aspects of Mozart's personality, but shows his more familiar side with great charm and persuasiveness.

The next Concerto, in D, K.451, is very different in general character from its two predecessors. It does not show the wayward imaginativeness of K.449 or the lyrical grace of K.450, but it has a first movement of great power, the slow movement is full of gently nostalgic charm, and the finale, though less attractive thematically than usual, is spirited and effective. The orchestra consists of flutes, oboes, horns, trumpets, drums and strings, and the massive opening tutti of the first movement exploits these resources fully. Again we meet in the first bar the martial rhythm already noticed in the Concerto for three pianos and in K.415. It is followed by an exhilarating passage over a tonic pedal that is frequently to be found towards the end of the exposition of the first movement of a Mannheim symphony or, at a later period, in a Rossini overture, but very rarely at so early a stage in a movement. Some aggressive descending scales in a dotted-note rhythm emphasise the strenuous character of the whole movement, which, for Mozart, has unusually little in the way of lyrical relief; the nearest approach is a pleasantly conversational little tune that is part of the second group, and is reminiscent of one of the themes in the first movement of the Sinfonia Concertante for violin and viola. Another unusual feature is the very close correspondence between the tutti and the exposition; there are none of the surprises that are usually to be found in the latter. Perhaps the most striking theme in the movement is that in Ex. 20 opposite. With its chromaticism this theme provides a striking contrast to the almost aggressively forthright character of the movement as a whole. The piano enters with a floridly decorated version of the opening theme, and throughout the movement it is used more for brilliant than for melodic writing. The development section, which is surprisingly short considering the size of the whole movement, grows very attractively from the final stages of the exposition, but becomes, as so often, less thematic and, as usually happens in such passages, the harmonic movement becomes broader and more meditative. The recapitulation has no particularly new features but Mozart's cadenza is very fine, especially at the moment when Ex. 20 is brought in against an entirely new background. The movement as a whole may to some music-lovers

Ex.20

inspire admiration rather than affection, largely owing to the paucity of the characteristic Mozartian melodic charm. But its structure, if comparatively conventional, is splendidly conceived, and there is a sense of powerful and inexorable logic that is perhaps more typical of Beethoven than of Mozart.

Of the authorship of the slow movement, on the other hand, there could be no doubt whatever. The gentle chromaticism of the main theme is particularly characteristic. It is in a simple ABACA rondo form, with sensitive variations of the main theme on its recurrences. These are concerned with texture rather than melodic elaboration, which could easily sound out of place in so intimate a movement. The first episode is in the dominant: the phrases are shorter than those of the main theme, which gives the impression of greater tension while towards the end they become more florid. The second episode, starting in the relative minor, is also built on short phrases at first, but a beautifully timed modulation to C major introduces a broad melody for the soloist against a very simple accompaniment. Mozart's sister found the piano part of this passage over bare and he sent her a more ornate version (Ex. 21). The decorated version would certainly have been more effective on the piano of Mozart's time, though on purely musical grounds it is possible to prefer his first thoughts. But in any case the very deliberate movement of the harmony gives the whole passage a wonderful spaciousness. After the last return of the main theme there is a coda which recalls phrases from the first episode. The scoring of this

Ex.21

movement is particularly attractive, the prominence of the woodwind producing a feeling of cool and ethereal calm. As so often in Mozart's rondos, the returns of the main theme are cunningly graded. The first, coming from the dominant, is done very simply in two bars: for the second more suspense is required – four bars of beautifully woven contrapuntal texture for the strings are answered by a descending passage for the woodwind, after which the piano quietly brings back the theme in a high register.

If the first movement of this work suggests Beethoven, the finale also has a strong kinship with another composer; 'too much Haydn and too little Mozart' was the severe comment of Einstein.[1] Coming after the particularly intimate slow movement it certainly seems rather impersonal, but, taken on its own terms, it is a lively and effective piece of music, rivalling the first movement in sustained energy. It is in a very clear-cut sonata rondo form. After the very sectional main theme there is a vigorous transitional passage starting in bare octaves. The theme of the first episode is very Haydnesque, but when the piano repeats it there are a few chromatic decorations more characteristic of Mozart. The main theme, which on its first appearance was, very exceptionally, played by the orchestra, now returns with each of its two strains given first to the piano and then to the orchestra. The central episode is very eventful; first a new and decidedly Mozartian theme in B minor, then the tune of the first episode, this time in a minor key, then a very attractive passage

1   Einstein, *op. cit.*

36

in which, as in the finale of K.450, the first two bars of the main theme glance quietly at several remote keys before returning to the tonic. After a varied return of the main theme and a recapitulation of the first episode in the tonic, there is a coda in 3/8 time, which makes use of both the main theme and that of the first episode. Between them comes a new idea which, surprisingly, has the last word in the vigorous final bars. If not one of the most immediately attractive of the piano concertos, K.451 remains a powerful and interesting work that certainly deserves to be better known.

But the Concerto in G, K.453, seems to have everything, being equally attractive to listeners and scholars alike. Mention has already been made of the rhythm of the opening bars of K.451, and it is interesting to see how Mozart was obsessed by it at this period. It is a rhythm that is liable to appear as a background, played by the brass, in many first movements in common time. But in four consecutive piano concertos it is more than that, being part of the first theme:

Ex.22

(a)

(b)

(c)

(d)

The four first movements however are very dissimilar in general character. That of K.451 is aggressively energetic, that of K.453 mellow and kindly and those of the other two are more mercurial and vivacious, sometimes with a touch of comedy. In K.453, Ex. 22b does not play a particularly important part as, although it makes an immediate impression, it is one of many themes. The tutti is, as usual, full of ideas. A leaping figure played by the woodwind leads to a wistful and appealing melody that eventually plays an important part in the second group. There is a brief but dramatic plunge into a remote key that foreshadows some of the remarkable modulations in the development section and a very characteristic phrase containing a poignant passing dissonance over a tonic pedal. Neither of these recur until after the recapitulation. The soloist enters with the first theme, and eventually the second group opens with a very graceful melody that was not heard in the tutti. But the wistful theme and other previous ideas return, all, of course, in the dominant. The very impressive development section appears to be quite nonthematic, though in its first stages there is a phrase of four crotchets that, as Tovey pointed out,[1] may be connected with four detached quavers that appeared at the mysterious plunge into E flat during the tutti. A very striking modulation to C minor introduces an entirely new phrase that gradually leads back to the recapitulation.

Mozart wrote two cadenzas for this movement between which there is little to choose, though the first, though less brilliant, is perhaps the more appealing. It is preceded and followed by passages that have not been heard since the opening tutti. The leaping figure that first appeared early in the movement asserts itself vigorously in the final bars.

The andante is in C major, and, for the first time since K.414, is in full sonata form, complete with opening tutti. Its unusual character can be felt at the end of the first phrase, which is followed by a pause; this immediately suggests the atmosphere of an operatic 'scena'. It is succeeded by a procession of ideas which all eventually form the second group. First, a dialogue for the woodwind, recalling a passage in the andante of the two-piano Sonata in D; then a more energetic phrase that does not recur until the recapitulation, and finally a few bars of extraordinary beauty and pathos in which major and minor seem to blend in an almost Schubertian way. The piano enters with the first theme but, again, after five bars it draws up for a pause.

The second group opens with a passionate theme in G minor that has not been heard before and comes with startling effect after the pause. The woodwind dialogue and the major-minor phrase appear in the dominant, and the development section opens with the first theme also in G. After the usual pause the piano enters in D minor, and goes

1 Sir Donald Tovey, *Essays in Musical Analysis*, vol. 3 (Oxford, 1936).

through a remarkable chain of modulations that lead further and further into the distance, almost settling in C sharp minor. The return from this sombre region is effected in four bars only, but with a strong sense of direction that covers the ground quickly without any suggestion of hesitation or fussiness.

In the recapitulation the G minor outburst with which the second group began now appears in E flat, sounding still more dramatic after the pause. The woodwind dialogue is followed by the energetic phrase that was omitted in the exposition. After the cadenza the first theme makes its final appearance and, for the first time, there is no pause; there are some delicate touches of chromaticism in both melody and harmony.

Finally the movement is rounded off beautifully by the major-minor phrase. Of the slightly earlier concerto slow movements that of K.449 comes nearest to this one but in the andante of the G major Concerto there is a far greater power and range of emotion. It is in fact one of the most original and deeply felt of all Mozart's slow movements.

Reference has already been made to Mozart's wonderful power of characterisation in his operas. It was this, coupled with his innate humanity and good taste, that enabled him to follow the heart-searching slow movement of this work with a light-hearted set of variations. There is a strong suggestion of Papageno in the theme, though the third and fourth bars of the second half give a glimpse of the subtler and more sensitive Mozart and when the piano enters for the first variation there are no traces of rusticity. For the remaining variations, as in K.450, each half is repeated in a varied form. In the second, the melody of the theme is unaltered, being played first by the orchestra and by the piano in the repeats. In the third, a dialogue for the woodwind is answered by a gracefully flowing passage for the piano. The fourth, in G minor, provides a striking contrast to the rest. Both orchestra and piano are in a sombre mood, the one austere and enigmatic, especially in the second half, and the other more agitated. For the fifth, both parties have recovered their spirits, the orchestra being boisterously cheerful and the piano, amiably elegant. This is followed, however, by a few bars of singularly beautiful texture leading to a half close.

The sequel is almost a complete movement in itself. It is immensely exhilarating, vividly suggesting the atmosphere of intrigue and excitement that is so characteristic of Italian comic opera. At first the orchestra dominates the scene, but the piano refuses to be left out and becomes increasingly voluble. Twice there is a brief but mysterious lull that seems to look back for a moment to the sombre atmosphere of the fourth variation. The theme itself appears at first to have been completely forgotten, but halfway through it dances in cheerfully at a quick pace, and at the end it appears in a shortened version with interruptions from the wind instruments. Finally the concerto ends with a few bars of lively repartee between piano and orchestra. Few of Mozart's works cover so wide a range of emotion as this concerto; the genial warmth of the first movement, the depth and intensity of the slow movement, and the comedy of the finale make a singularly satisfying whole. Trumpets and drums would not have fitted with the generally intimate character of the work, and the orchestra is like that of K.450, except that the flute occurs in all three movements. Throughout the work the colouring is of great beauty and charm.

The Concerto in B flat, K.456, has on the whole been underrated and under-performed; it has not quite the warmth and richness of the G major Concerto and, apart from its slow movement, it might at first acquaintance give the impression of being a slight and superficial work. But behind its high spirits there is a wayward imaginativeness which can be felt in the opening tutti. After the already quoted opening theme (Ex. 22c), a more strenuous idea appears, after which there is a sudden and unexpected lull leading to a cadence in B flat minor. Both this and the lively little tune for woodwind that follows it prove to be part of the second group of the exposition. Towards the end of the tutti there is a light-hearted fanfare that plays a very important part in the development section. As in the G major Concerto, the soloist enters with the main theme and the exposition proceeds on much the same lines. As so often, the second group begins with a new theme for the piano that has not been heard before. The mysterious B flat minor passage appears now in F minor, and is all the more impressive for being swathed in arpeggios played by the piano.

The development section has not the extraordinary spaciousness of that of the first movement of the G major Concerto. The piano starts in a floridly lyrical vein, but this gives place to a passage of light texture in which Ex. 23 is accompanied by detached notes on the strings and scales on the piano. The more lyrical mood returns, however, and soon a feeling of suspense is caused when the piano plays arpeggios supported by sustained chords on the strings. It is clear at this point that the return of the main theme is imminent. But before this happens there is a mysterious touch of chromaticism very similar to the equivalent passage in the first movement of K.449. The recapitulation is fairly regular, the final bars being identical with those of the opening tutti. Mozart wrote two cadenzas for this movement, of which the second is perhaps the more interesting, though both contain some very characteristic touches.

The slow movement is a set of variations, and the general plan is in many ways similar to that of the G major Concerto's finale. In both sets the first variation is a delicately accompanied piano solo; the next three are double variations in which the piano plays the more prominent part in the varied repeat. But in atmosphere the two sets could hardly be more dissimilar. That of K.456 is in G minor and full of the elegiac melancholy so characteristic of Mozart's music in that key. The theme itself is far less simple than those in K.450 and K.453; it has more in common with that of the variations in the slightly later String Quartet in A, K.464. In both themes every phrase begins halfway through the bar, and the texture has more subtle detail than is usual in a theme intended for variations. In the Quartet movement there is a wealth of new and attractive melodic invention in the variations; in the Concerto the melody of the theme is more prominent, though less so in the varied repeats, where there is some delicate ornamentation. In the third variation there is a strong contrast between an angry orchestra and a wistful piano; the final bars, with the piano playing in a low register, are very impressive. The fourth, in G major, is the freest and the most beautiful; in its context it has a profoundly nostalgic effect prophetic of a similar moment in the slow movement of Schubert's 'Death and the Maiden' Quartet.

In the last variation there are no repeats and the melody of the theme is played by the orchestra, with the piano providing a very stormy background. The coda is dominated by the rhythm of the first four notes of the theme, which is transferred from one instrument to another with almost hypnotic persistence. The fluctuations between major and minor, again, have a foretaste of Schubert. Attention has been drawn to a superficial resemblance between the opening bars of the theme and those of Barbarina's song in *Figaro*, but surely its general mood comes far nearer to the deeply moving G minor aria sung by Pamina in *Die Zauberflöte*.

The finale has obvious resemblances to that of K.450. In one of the subsidiary themes of the former there is a suggestion of a hunting horn; this is even stronger in the main theme of K.456 and permeates the whole movement. The high spirits are less urbane and aristocratic, there is less concern with brilliant and elaborate keyboard writing and, in the central episode, a more wayward imaginativeness. It is a sonata rondo with the usual wealth of ideas. The first episode opens with a delightfully voluble transitional theme which moves in a leisurely way to the dominant, where there is a new and equally lively melody to which a cross rhythm gives a decided touch of comedy. In due course the main theme returns, and leads to the very remarkable second episode. The music modulates to the remote key of B minor; the woodwind change from 6/8 to 2/4, but the piano plays arpeggios in the original tempo. Then the piano also changes to 2/4, with a new melody. The nearest approach to this mixture of time signatures in Mozart's music is in the last movement of the Oboe Quartet, written some years earlier, in which at one point the oboe plays in common time, while the strings are still in 6/8. A return from a remote key usually takes longer than the journey to it; here it is done spaciously and deliberately, but leads not to the main theme but to the transitional passage. After the first episode has been recapitulated in the tonic the main theme returns for the last time and the movement ends punctually and precisely.

Looking back for a moment at the concerto as a whole, the andante is certainly the most striking part, but the outer movements, in addition to the vivid contrast that they provide, have far more beneath their liveliness and charm than is immediately apparent. It is interesting, as Professor Girdlestone has pointed out,[1] to reflect that the work of Mozart that came nearest to this concerto in point of time was the stormy and passionate Piano Sonata in C minor. This fact does not merely illustrate the wide range of Mozart's genius, but also suggests that to him, as to Beethoven, there was a special fascination in doing two very dissimilar things within a short space of time.

Of the piano concertos written in 1784, K.459 in F is the most exuberant and of the more sombre aspects of Mozart's personality there is hardly a trace. Even the second movement is marked 'allegretto' and the outer movements are characterised by an exhilarating combination of high spirits and technical resourcefulness. In the first movement the very precise and square-cut opening tune, beginning with Ex. 22d, brings an atmosphere of complete informality and, though it is one of Mozart's longest and most solidly built first movements, it has none of the monumental character of that of K.503. The tutti contains the usual procession of ideas, two of which are not heard again until the final stage of the movement. But, as so often happens, the most distinctive theme of the second group is kept in reserve for the soloist to play in the exposition.

When writing this movement Mozart's invention was particularly

1   Girdlestone, *op. cit.*

prolific and there is one pleasant transitional tune that is completely abandoned after its appearance. But as the movement proceeds it is more and more evident that the main theme is far the most important character in the plot. Throughout the second group it appears frequently against an astonishing variety of harmonic backgrounds. In the development section of the first movement of a piano concerto Mozart's procedure is totally unpredictable, as we have seen; sometimes he feels no obligation to make use of already existing material. In the first movement of K.459, having done so much with the main theme during the exposition, it would not have been surprising if he had ignored it in the development section. But it becomes increasingly insistent, appearing first in a long sequence against a background of quaver triplets played by the piano and then in a fierce argument with the piano, then, after a few bars of passage work, it returns and leads the music back firmly from D minor to F for the recapitulation. This has some interesting changes resulting from the return of a theme not heard since the tutti. Mozart's cadenza for this movement introduces various themes with masterly skill; the reference to the main theme is particularly attractive, and might have suggested to Beethoven one of the loveliest themes in his G major Concerto.

The use of a tempo as fast as allegretto for a central movement is unusual, though Haydn does so for the slow movement, also in C major, of his Quartet in G, Op. 54 no. 1. The two movements, both in 6/8, are not unalike, though Haydn's has some stranger harmonic half-lights. The unusual phraseology of Mozart's theme (Ex. 23, below) is particularly charming, and suited to the leisurely atmosphere of the movement.

Ex.23

Allegretto

It is in sonata form without development, but the opening tutti contains some very expressive music that never returns; this suggests that Mozart might originally have had a more elaborate plan in mind. The piano enters with the main theme gracefully decorated, but soon moves to an eventful second group. Rather surprisingly this does not start with a new theme, but instead Mozart introduces, much as Haydn might have done, a delightful dialogue for flute, bassoon and piano on a variant of the main theme. When this has run its course a new melody in G minor is shared between first oboe and flute; the piano then repeats it and the music continues in a vein of deep pathos that is particularly moving in contrast to the serene and idyllic mood of the rest. But the major key soon returns, and an elegant passage leads back for the recapitulation.

In the recapitulation the opening orchestral passage is omitted; the first theme is slightly varied, and the texture of the contrapuntal dialogue at the beginning of the second group is considerably more elaborate than before. This time the first oboe, not the flute, takes part in it. There are also modifications in the plaintive minor key passage, to suit the compass of the instruments. Throughout the movement the writing for the woodwind is particularly sensitive, and in the coda they answer each other delightfully with scale passages in a manner very similar to the final bars of Susanna's 'Deh vieni' from *Figaro*. This particular serenade-like vein never reappears in the piano concertos; in Mozart's later instrumental music the nearest approach is the slow movement of the Prague Symphony. But there are several instances in the operas, for which this very lovely movement may well have provided inspiration.

The finale of this concerto matches the first movement in its abounding vitality and technically it is one of the most brilliant things that Mozart ever wrote. Like the finales of K.175 and K.449, it is concerned with the coexistence of contrapuntal and harmonic elements, and it achieves this triumphantly. It is basically in a sonata rondo form and opens with a lively dialogue in which the two strains of the very spritely main theme are played first by piano and then by orchestra. A long orchestral tutti follows, which contains first a vigorous fugal passage on a new theme, then an anticipation in the tonic of a variant of the first theme that turns out to be an important feature of the first episode, and then a more placid cadential theme that does not recur till near the end of the movement. The piano then re-enters with a very pleasant new tune which, rather disappointingly, never reappears. The first episode contains the variant of the first theme already mentioned, and a very spritely new tune of a rather Haydnesque kind:

Ex.24

It also contains the fugal theme in a rather less fugal texture. After a return of the main theme the second episode bursts out in a longer fugal passage in D minor. Here the original fugal theme and the first bars of the main theme are used as subject and counter-subject, with most exhilarating results. Eventually the contrapuntal excitement subsides, but without the slightest feeling of incongruity, and the first episode is recapitulated. The first theme does not return until after the cadenza, of which Mozart has written a very lively and effective specimen. On its final reappearance the first theme is accompanied by triplets, a new feature, but this soon gives way to the quiet cadential theme that was last heard at the end of the first tutti. Finally the movement ends with spirited exchanges between piano and orchestra. This concerto as a whole has a remarkable unity of mood. Mozart obviously regarded the work as essentially a comedy and felt that, although a touch of wistful regret in the second movement would not be out of place, a deeply felt slow movement like those of K.453 or K.488 would not fit in with the general scheme. But in its very individual way this concerto is an undoubted masterpiece and, with its robust vitality, it provides a splendid climax to the series of six concertos that Mozart wrote within an astonishingly short space of time in 1784.

Vienna, 1785–91

But Mozart was still to write eight more concertos, which cover a wider emotional range. The first of the three written in 1785, K.466 in D minor, is different in atmosphere from any that he had written before. The String Quartet in the same key, K.421, has something of the same dark and foreboding mood in its opening bars, but in the concerto it finds fuller expression and is far more explosive. The first *forte*, when the smouldering tension of the main theme comes out into the open, is an electrifying moment that can never lose its power to excite. If there is here a foretaste of *Don Giovanni*, the music can with equal justice be said to stem from some things in *Idomeneo*, such as Electra's D minor aria. The quieter moments in this tutti are equally impressive. There is an apparently simple theme that for its first two bars is in F major, but always moves away; here it soon returns to D minor but when it appears in the exposition as part of the second group it returns to F major, though it would not have done so in the tutti. There is also the very characteristic and touching cadential passage near the end, which prepares the way beautifully for the entry of the piano:

Ex.25

This is the purest Mozartian lyricism but in view of the general trend of the movement, it obviously cannot be allowed to expand for long. Soon the first theme of the movement returns and after four bars the piano provides an agitated background of semiquavers. Eventually the second group begins with the theme already mentioned, which leads to a gentler and more relaxed tune which has not been heard before. It is played first by the piano and then by the woodwind. But soon reminiscences of the first tutti appear, this time in a major key, but restless and energetic. Eventually the exposition ends with the cadential theme, which, as before, leads to Ex. 25, in F major. This marks the beginning of the development, which is eventful, though not particularly long. Ex. 25 appears twice more, in G minor and E flat, but is always cut short by reminiscences of the opening.

A broadly sequential passage follows, with the piano playing agitated arpeggios and the menacing four-note figure that has played so impor-

tant a part in the opening theme becoming very insistent. After a period
of suspense the recapitulation begins. Surprisingly, the second group
starts in F major with the theme that first appeared in the tutti; this
time, inevitably, it returns to D minor as it did on its first appearance.
The rest of the second group follows in D minor, sounding far more
sombre than it had done before; the quiet and mysterious end of the
movement is particularly impressive.

For the second movement there is no indication of tempo; the title
'Romanze' obviously indicates a gently flowing pace. Its construction is
very simple, perhaps almost naïve compared with that of some of the
more highly organised slow movements. The main theme, very characteristic of Mozart in its delicate chromatic touches, expands in a very
leisurely way, with constant interchanges between piano and orchestra.
The first episode is a kind of cavatina for the piano. It is still in the tonic
key, and there is no attempt at any vivid contrast, but the melodic
phrases are broader than those of the main theme, and the harmony
moves with greater deliberation, the orchestra playing a very simple
accompaniment of repeated chords. Gradually the music moves to the
dominant and the episode ends with a cadential passage already heard at
the end of the first section. After a shortened return of the main theme
there is a far more contrasted episode in G minor, with a constant flow of
agitated triplets for the piano. This certainly introduces an element of
drama into a movement that might otherwise seem over-placid; it is
most effective if played without any quickening of the pulse. The grad-
ual return to the peaceful mood of the rest of the movement is beautifully contrived. After the final appearance of the main theme in its
complete form there is a short coda of great charm and simplicity. As in
many of Mozart's slow movements, the writing for the woodwind is
particularly attractive. The charm of the main theme and the arresting
contrast provided by the second episode make this one of the most
immediately appealing of the slow movements in the Mozart piano concertos, though there are others that may make a more lasting impression.

The fiery and energetic finale provides a magnificent counterpart to
the darker colouring of the first movement. The opening theme has a
tremendous impetus resulting initially from the rising arpeggio, a
startlingly aggressive version of the conventional 'Mannheim rocket':

Ex.26

When the piano has played this, there is a long orchestral tutti which contains a very powerful passage that, surprisingly, does not return. Against a background of rapid repeated notes a slowly rising chromatic scale is played canonically over a dominant pedal; this is answered by a descending scale in canon over a tonic pedal. It gives the impression of immense energy firmly guided by a kind of inexorable logic. When this outburst has run its full course the piano re-enters with a gentle theme: Ex.27

This theme has a strong likeness to Ex.25 in the first movement. It is soon brushed aside by the main theme, which leads to what proves to be the first episode of a sonata rondo. It has two contrasting elements, an agitated theme in F minor, and a very gay one in F major, which has, however, some characteristic touches of chromaticism. After the expected return of the main theme the second episode is really a development section in some ways very similar to that of the first movement; the lyrical Ex. 30 appears in various keys but is never allowed to continue for long.

It is never safe to predict in what order Mozart will reintroduce his material in a rondo of this kind. Here the central episode is followed by a recapitulation of the first, with everything in D minor. After the cadenza, the first theme returns and is not heard again. The coda, in D major, is concerned with the second theme of the first episode. It is played twice and then, after reminiscences of the first tutti, it returns in a different version, ending with a cheerfully matter-of-fact phrase played by trumpets and horns. This becomes more insistent and the movement ends in a mood prophetic of the final sextet in *Don Giovanni*. The last bars of the piano part are surprising; it seems to end in mid air, on an unresolved chord. Despite the presence of trumpets and drums, the end of the D minor Concerto is not exuberant in the manner of the two previous ones; it aims rather at relaxation after tension, as Beethoven did in an odder and more unpredictable way at the end of the Quartet in F minor, Op. 95. In the following year, when he wrote the C minor Concerto, Mozart maintained an unrelievedly sombre atmosphere in the final stages.

The Concerto in C, K.467, contains in its first movement the cere-monial atmosphere characteristic of other works in this key. The stealthily martial opening is not unlike that of K.415, but the present movement is a far more convincing structure. The whole of the orchestra is employed in the first eight bars, the statement of the theme by the strings being neatly rounded off by the other instruments; the quiet use of the trumpets and drums is prophetic of *Die Zauberflöte*. The first two bars of the main theme are not only easily recognisable, but are equally effective as a bass or as material for contrapuntal imitation:

Ex.28

The tutti contains two ideas that do not reappear till the recapitulation; one, quietly processional, and the other curiously menacing:

Ex.29

The entry of the soloist is preceded by a charming dialogue for the woodwind. After some lively flourishes from the piano, the first theme reappears; the first four bars are played by the strings, and the piano, having played a trill over them, finishes the sentence on its own. On the way to the second group there is a passing idea that, on paper, immediately suggests the opening of the G minor Symphony, though the considerably slower tempo makes the resemblance seem far less in performance. There is, as usual, a gracefully flowing theme for the piano in the second group, which ends with material already heard in the tutti. The development section opens with a new idea, the second bar of which recalls that of the main theme; soon however it is submerged in arpeggios, and the main part of this section consists of those passages that frequently occur at this stage in the first movements of Mozart's concertos; a leisurely sequence with slowly moving harmony but with rapid semiquaver passages on the piano. After a certain amount of effectively prolonged suspense the recapitulation starts; some transitional material is omitted, and other ideas not heard since the tutti are recalled. In view of its generally massive character, the final bars of the movement are surprisingly playful; the strings appear to be trying, with some difficulty, to remember the main theme.

The andante is one of the most strikingly individual of Mozart's slow movements. It gives the general impression of a broad and almost unbroken stream of lyrical melody against a background of triplets. But it proves after analysis to be in sonata form, though such is the continuity of mood that the formal landmarks are hardly noticeable. For the first time since the slow movement of K.238, the strings are muted; in the opening tutti the main melody, which consists at first of three-bar phrases, leads to a remarkably poignant passage with surprisingly sharp dissonances, which eventually appears, in a more ornate form, as the second subject. After a short development there is a quietly thrilling moment when the first subject returns for recapitulation in the unexpected key of A flat.

In this movement, if anywhere, Mozart can be seen as the fore-runner of the nineteenth century. The dissonances in the second subject have a vivid foretaste of Schumann and the way in which they gently melt into the major key is equally prophetic of Schubert. The variety of phrase-lengths gives a fascinatingly rhapsodic feeling to the music and there is much unobtrusive skill in the way in which the background of throbbing triplets is shifted periodically from one tone-colour to another. It is doubtful whether any composer but Mozart could, without any feeling of anticlimax, have concluded this atmospheric and romantically coloured movement with six bars of extreme, almost childlike simplicity.

The finale, like that of K.459, is a lively sonata rondo in 2/4 time, but in general character the two movements are not very alike. The F major Rondo has greater variety of material, a stronger rhythmic drive and the special exhilaration resulting from the fugal passages. The finale of K.467 is more elegant, as can be guessed from its main theme:

Ex.30

Allegro vivace assai

This has an attractive flexibility resulting from the fact that its phrases always begin on an unaccented bar. There are some new and attractive ideas in the first episode, one lively and rhythmic, and the other chromatic in a very Mozartian way. But the most striking part of the movement is the central episode, which is built entirely on the main theme. After a very neat modulation to A major it appears in a more lyrical vein; eventually the first 1 ½ bars are detached from the rest, and become the subject of a heated argument. Shortly before the theme returns in its original form there is a passage that recalls, consciously or not, Ex. 29 from the first movement. The first episode is recapitulated in the usual way and there is a brilliant coda, the main theme asserting itself to the last. With all its delightful qualities this finale does not quite rise to the very high level of the other two movements, but something very special would be needed for an adequate sequel to the wonderful andante.

The third of the 1785 piano concertos, K.482, in E flat, is a large and imposing work, notable especially for the variety and richness of its orchestration; this has a particularly mellow quality resulting from the substitution of clarinets for oboes. After the ceremonious opening bars, this quality can be felt strongly in the delightful conversation between the flute, the two clarinets and the two bassoons, with the violins playing a counter-melody and the horns joining in for the cadence. Shortly after this comes a tune so immediately memorable that Mozart can afford to keep it in reserve till its return in the recapitulation:

Ex.31

The graceful cadential phrase with which the tutti ends seems to indicate that the ceremonious atmosphere of the opening is only one of the many facets of this movement. In the early stages of the exposition Mozart seems to have in his head more ideas than he needs. The very attractive passage with which the piano enters is never again alluded to directly, and later on, as in the first movement of K.467, a passionate theme in the dominant minor appears for a moment and no more. In both passages the theme is introduced by a rising scale in octaves, with an effect that is temporarily startling, but seems to have no connection with later events. Perhaps these passing ideas would have been used by Mozart in his cadenzas, which, in the case of these two works, have unfortunately not survived. The main theme of the second group is very simple, though when repeated in a varied form it suggests a possible, though probably accidental connection with the phrase with which the piano first entered. It makes a brief appearance in the development section, which is otherwise entirely non-thematic with the piano playing rapid passages against slowly moving harmonies. In the recapitulation there are some very effective changes in the scoring and a delightful moment when Ex. 31 appears in an extended form just as we are expecting the main theme of the second group.

The andante has some particularly interesting and unusual features, perhaps the most notable being its varied colour scheme. The long and very beautiful main theme is played by the strings with violins muted; it is then repeated in a varied form by the piano, the strings providing an occasional background. The first episode is scored for woodwind and horns; then the theme, or rather another variation of it, is played by piano and strings. For the second episode the first flute and the first bassoon have a graceful duet supported by the strings; then another variation which is a dialogue between orchestra and piano, followed by a coda.

The general scheme comes near to the twentieth-century idea of a 'concerto for orchestra'. The combination of elements of the rondo and variation forms is also unusual. The theme itself is remarkable for its rhythmic freedom and after its solemn colouring the very sensitive decorations by the piano in the first variation are particularly appealing. The first episode is very similar to certain things in the wind serenades and its quiet richness of sound looks ahead to the orchestral introduction to the duet 'Secondate, aurette amiche' in *Così fan tutte*. The massive texture of the second variation and the delicacy of the second episode are well contrasted, but the most striking parts of the movement are the last variation and coda. In the former, as in one of the variations in K.456, the piano pleads gently with an angry orchestra. A new idea, which appears over a menacing trill, plays an important part in the coda:

Ex.32

This is of some length and towards the end a phrase from the first episode, which had originally sounded demurely playful, now returns in C minor, with deeply melancholy effect.

The cheerful finale brings us down to earth, but with great charm and lightness of touch. The jauntiness of the main theme could easily tempt the incautious to an excessively quick pace, which would lessen the effect of many details, and reduce the semiquaver passages to the empty brilliance of a musical-box. As in the first movement, Mozart is teeming with ideas and although this finale is in a far more light-hearted mood than the Allegro, it is at least as well organised as a structure. It is a sonata rondo, but on a large and leisurely scale. Between the main theme and the first episode are two subsidiary melodies, both in the tonic. One is given to the first clarinet, the second providing a delightful murmuring accompaniment; the other is played by the piano against detached chords.

The melody of the first episode is equally attractive; after the return of the main theme the music appears to be moving towards C minor for the second episode, but instead it changes direction very impressively and pauses on the dominant seventh of A flat. In this key there is a central episode, marked 'andantino cantabile' and reminiscent in some ways of a similar passage in the finale of the early Concerto in E flat, K.271. But it is in a slower tempo and more direct and clear-cut in its expressiveness. Here again there is a foretaste of *Così fan tutte*.

As in the earlier movement, the passage leading back to E flat is very picturesquely scored. The main theme, on its return, is slightly altered melodically, and when it makes its final appearance after the recapitulation of the first episode, there are some delightful harmonic changes. Mozart may have felt that so simple a theme might pall with too much note-for-note repetition. The two subsidiary melodies both reappear in the coda; the second is played, as before, over detached chords, and also under sustained chords on the woodwind, giving it an almost dreamlike quality. Apart from its exceptional wealth of contrasting ideas, the most notable characteristic of this concerto is a kind of luxuriant leisureliness; it is perhaps significant that Professor Girdlestone[1] and A. Hyatt King[2] have both described it as 'queenly'.

THE THREE CONCERTOS OF 1786 (K.488, K.491, K.503)

If K.482 looks back in some ways to K.271, the Concerto in A, K.488, has a still stronger kinship with K.414. This is especially true of the two first movements, which have the same flowing melodiousness, though the latter movement is the more thoughtful of the two. There are still clarinets instead of oboes, but no trumpets or drums. As in K.414, the first subject is followed by a more energetic passage, and then by the main theme of the second group, which, especially in the later concertos, is usually kept in reserve for the piano in the exposition. The exposition follows the tutti with unusual closeness, but the extra-

1 Girdlestone, *op. cit.*
2 A. Hyatt King, *The Concerto* (Harmondsworth, 1952).

ordinary charm of the thematic material and the genial and sunny atmosphere of the music prevent the slightest suspicion of monotony. But there is a surprise in store. The cadential phrase at the end of the tutti does not reappear, but at the final stage of the exposition a sudden silence ushers in a new idea of great beauty, still in the dominant, which leads imperceptibly into the development section:

Ex.33

This is dominated by the new phrase, or rather by its rhythm, which is interrupted from time to time by a semiquaver figure, but becomes increasingly persistent, leading the music through a number of keys. In the recapitulation there is more work for Ex. 33. On its first appearance it had been played by the strings and repeated in a varied form by the piano; now it is played by the piano and continued by the woodwind, the piano playing a lively counterpoint; it also makes a brief return shortly before the cadenza. Apart from its intrinsic beauty the fact that its appearances are preceded by a silence makes them particularly effective. The cadenza that Mozart wrote for this movement has been criticised for its brevity and slightness, but he may well have thought that for so lyrical a movement anything more portentous would be out of place. The cadential phrase that ended the opening tutti returns in the coda and the movement ends neatly and informally.

The second movement is headed 'Adagio' in the autograph, not 'Andante' as in all the subsequent editions. It is interesting to note that both Mozart and Beethoven used the key of F sharp minor only once, and in both cases for a slow movement of great emotional depth. The mood of Mozart's movement had been foreshadowed twelve years before in the very touching little adagio of the early Piano Sonata in F, K.280, and there is even a hint of the main theme. But in 1786 Mozart's style had developed immeasurably; he had come to think in longer and more varied sentences, and his harmony had become richer and more subtle. In Beethoven's one F sharp minor movement, the adagio of the Piano Sonata in B flat, Op. 106, the wonderful modulation to G major during the course of the main theme may have been inspired by the ninth and tenth bars of Mozart's movement. After the piano has played the beautifully delicate first theme the orchestra plays another which is broader and lends itself readily to contrapuntal treatment:

Ex.34

A few months later, by a curious coincidence (it can hardly have been more), Mozart used this theme, in the major and utterly different in mood, in the finale of his Sonata for piano duet in F, K.497. A transitional passage for piano seems to grow inevitably from what came before it and leads very deliberately to the central section in A major. This has a modestly ornate melody, picturesquely scored, which brings no more than a passing relief to the melancholy mood of the movement. In due course the first section is repeated, but with modifications. There is a remarkable coda in which the piano plays a series of widely spread sustained notes against a pizzicato background. Whether these notes represent what Mozart would actually have played, or whether he would have elaborated the passage in performance is a question about which opinions vary; in any case no elaboration can be more impressive than what Mozart wrote, if played on a piano with a sufficiently rich singing tone.

The finale is an immensely exhilarating sonata rondo with, even for Mozart, an exceptionally rich store of melodies. After the very lively main tune, there is an orchestral tutti which introduces a new theme and continues for some time. Towards the end there is a passing glance at F sharp minor which, intentionally or not, is reminiscent of a similar moment in the opening tutti of the first movement. The first episode opens with another tune, more graceful and leisurely than either of the other two. This leads to E major but, when this is fully established, a new melody appears in E minor, which goes through some striking modulations before returning to the major. After some brilliant and energetic writing, yet another theme occurs; it amuses itself by running cheerfully up and down the scale of E major. It is at first played by the piano, but before long the orchestra cannot refrain from joining in. Eventually the main theme returns and is followed by the central episode, which contains two new ideas. One, in F sharp minor, is passionate and voluble and the other, in D major, more homely and equable. When these have run their course there is a return, not of the main theme but of the graceful melody that opened the first episode. This time it does not lead to E but remains in A, in which key, major or minor, the rest of the material reappears. The main theme in due course makes its final return, but there is still much more to come. The long tutti that followed the first theme at the beginning of the movement now returns, extended by an interruption from the scale-running tune from the first episode. Eventually the end comes briskly and punctually. As in the finale of the early E flat Concerto, K.271, there is here a highly satisfying combination of ebullient energy and spaciousness of movement and design. In company with that of the F major Concerto, K.459, it is Mozart's most consistently exhilarating concerto finale, and it provides a splendid climax to one of his most delightful and lovable works.

It has already been suggested that Mozart was sometimes fascinated by the idea of writing very dissimilar works in a short space. There could be no better instance of this than the fact that K.488 was followed so soon by the Piano Concerto in C minor, K.491. Mozart's works in that key tend to open with a defiant gesture; the Piano Sonata and the Serenade for wind are familiar instances. This atmosphere is at once felt in the magnificent opening theme of K.491, but it is all the more impressive for being at first stated quietly:

Ex.35

Its two most important features are the rising leap in the fourth bar, and the rhythm of bars five and six, which is liable to appear in many contexts. The tutti is dominated by the sombre opening; there are two subsidiary ideas; a dialogue of great beauty based on descending scales over a very simple harmonic basis, and an aggressive passage, also concerned with descending scales, but in a fierce dotted-note rhythm.

Neither of these play any part in the second group. The piano, as in the D minor Concerto, enters with a gentle cantabile theme, but Ex. 35 soon returns and leads to the second group in E flat. This contains two new themes of which the second has a melodic similarity to Ex. 24 from the finale of the F major Concerto:

Ex.36

This resemblance is worth quoting if only to demonstrate its superficiality. Ex. 35 appears in E flat minor, and the second group is rounded off by a passage built on bars five and six, with the leaps falling instead of rising. The development section, like that of the D minor Concerto, opens with the lyrical theme with which the piano first entered. Ex. 35 appears in F minor, and the passage that follows is dominated by bars five and six, with an unbroken flow of semiquavers played by the piano.

After a sequential dialogue for piano and orchestra of the kind that frequently occurs in the development sections of these concertos, the recapitulation is ushered in by stormy scale passages prophetic of Schubert's Piano Sonata in C minor. Here Mozart is very free in his procedure; the two themes of the second group return in reverse order, both in C minor. Then, in a richer texture than before, comes a passage from the opening tutti containing the dialogue referred to already. All this is in a comparatively subdued mood, but before long the main theme makes a very forcible entry, leading to the pause for the cadenza, at which Mozart, intentionally or not, gives no indication for a trill. After the cadenza another passage from the tutti returns, culminating with the descending scales in dotted notes, and finally the movement ends quietly, the piano playing arpeggios against muttered reminders of the rhythm of bars five and six.

After so complex and stormy a movement, the gentle and clear-cut larghetto provides a welcome relief. It is in a simple ABACA rondo form with coda and is full of the quiet warmth that is generally characteristic of Mozart's slow movements in E flat. The main theme has a child-like character which was recaptured many years later by Beethoven in the first movement of his Piano Sonata in E flat, Op. 27 no. 1. The two episodes, in C minor and A flat respectively, produce just the right degree of contrast with the theme and with each other. Neither stand out as vividly as the second episode in the 'Romanze' of the D minor Concerto, but the general effect is more satisfactory and the references to the second episode in the coda are particularly happy. With all its simplicity of manner, this movement is full of subtle details. During its course the first bar of the main theme appears in three different rhythmic guises, and on one occasion the rhythm of the third bar is also changed. The existence of these distinctions should discourage players from introducing melodic decorations which would obliterate them. There are also variations in harmony and orchestration. On its last appearance the theme is very richly scored, the second bar being doubled at the upper octave by flute, with striking effect. Both episodes contain two strains of equal length, which are played by the wind and repeated in a varied form by piano and strings. This movement may well have been a special favourite of Mozart's as, three years later, he wrote another which was extraordinarily similar – the adagio of the Piano Sonata in B flat, K.570. Inevitably it cannot command the same variety of colour as the concerto movement, but its musical content is equally, if not more, beautiful.

For the finale Mozart returns, for the last time in the piano concertos, to the variation form. The theme is very simple, but with curious, menacing undertones which become more ominous as the movement proceeds. In the first variation the piano plays a decorated version of the melody, against a simple orchestral background. The remaining variations, except the last, have varied repeats, but in most of them the melody of the theme is not far away. In the second it is obscured, though not destroyed, by rapid passages played by the piano in the repeats. In the third it stands out clearly in an aggressive march rhythm. It can still be felt, though less obviously, in the fourth which is in A flat and in a gently playful mood. The fifth, in C minor again, is concerned more with flowing contrapuntal texture, though in the repeats the melody, still in a marchlike rhythm, is more prominent. The sixth, in C major, is the freest and could more suitably be described as an interlude. As in the episodes of the slow movement, the two halves are played by wind and repeated by piano and strings. In the seventh, which has no repeats, the theme, slightly simplified, is accompanied by running passages on the piano. The eighth, in 6/8 time, is played by the piano alone, and the melody, as in the first variation, is decorated by very expressive chromatics. It is followed at once by a long and passionate coda; the D flat in the last few bars of the theme, which has become increasingly insistent during the previous variation, breaks out into:

Ex.37

This passage was much admired by Beethoven, and its influence can be felt in the finale of the *Appassionata* Sonata. Opinions have differed on the extent to which Mozart can be considered a tragic composer. Tovey denies the claim, though he is generally appreciative, and describes the C minor Concerto as sublime.[1] Personal reactions are bound to differ; it is worth recalling that a phrase in the first movement of the early String Quartet in D minor, K.173, which Saint-Foix described as 'un gémissement désespéré',[2] was likened by T. F. Dunhill, in his *Musical Pilgrim* volume on the quartets,[3] to the clucking of a hen. But surely the C minor Concerto has a truly tragic quality. Its greatness makes its effect less immediately than that of the D minor Concerto, but in the long run it is the finer work.

If K.491 is a tragedy, its successor, K.503, in C, written shortly after *Figaro*, can only be described as an epic. It employs a large orchestra, though less so than K.491, where there are both oboes and clarinets, the latter making their last appearance in the piano concertos. The first movement of K.503 has an astonishing breadth and spaciousness. Its air of formality is misleading, as what appear to be purely conventional gestures are liable at any moment to digress into unexpected paths. This can be seen early in the opening tutti, where, after a very ceremonious start, the music quietly glances towards C minor. A striking sequential passage is built on a rhythmic figure, which plays a very important part in the movement:

Ex.38

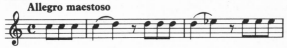

Here it soon leads to a powerful climax in the key of the dominant, a most unusual procedure at this stage. In K.449, the main theme of the second group appears for a short time in the dominant during the tutti, after which the music floats quietly back to the tonic. But here the dominant is emphasised with much panache. Ex. 38, deprived of its last note, introduces:

Ex.39

1 Tovey, *op. cit.*, vol. 2.
2 Saint-Foix and Wyzeva, *Mozart, sa vie musicale et son oeuvre* (Paris, 1912).
3 T. F. Dunhill, *Mozart – The Quartets* (Oxford, 1927).

This seems to be a premonition, in a minor key, of Papageno's 'Ein mädchen oder weibchen'. It is at once repeated in the major against a simple but sonorous background, including trumpets and drums playing quietly. There is a very similar passage in the tutti of the first movement of Beethoven's Piano Concerto in E flat. Other ideas follow, some ceremonious, and some more lyrical; the rhythm of Ex. 38, now complete, returns in a more melodious form. The entry of the soloist is highly original; at first it completes the sentences of the orchestra shyly and unobtrusively, and then becomes increasingly voluble. When it has said its say the exposition starts in the ceremonious mood of the tutti, but before long it moves with almost Schubertian informality to a very attractive lyrical passage for the piano in E flat. This proves, of course, to be part of a roundabout journey to the dominant, where the second group begins. Its first phrase looks back to Ex. 14 from K.415.

Ex.40

The rhythm of Ex. 38 makes itself felt and eventually the exposition ends with the passage that appeared, also in G major, during the tutti. Here, however, it has a far greater sense of finality.

The opening of the development section is a very striking moment. The incomplete version of Ex. 38, as in the tutti, ushers in Ex. 39, as before, but it now appears not in C minor but in E minor and, though apparently the simplest and most naïve theme in the movement, it now proceeds to take charge of the development. As it goes through a variety of keys the texture becomes increasingly elaborate; eventually this gives place to the usual passage of suspense before the recapitulation. In this, as usual, there are new adventures. The E flat melody reappears with attractive harmonic changes, leading to C major' Ex. 40 appears and is followed by Ex. 39 in the C major colouring in which it appeared in the tutti. Otherwise things proceed regularly till the cadenza, after which this large and eventful design is completed by a return of the final stages of the first tutti.

The andante is less intimate than some of Mozart's later slow movements, but it has much beauty of a serene and statuesque kind. For the last time in the concertos we meet a slow movement in sonata form with an opening tutti; here, however, there is no development section. In some ways this movement looks ahead to the andante of the 'Jupiter'

Symphony. They both open with broadly designed paragraphs that consist of a series of ideas rather than a continuous stream of melody. But in the symphonic movement there is a strong undercurrent of agitation whereas here the atmosphere is Olympian and comparatively detached. Its beauty lies less in its themes, which have not in themselves any notable distinction, than in the way in which they are arranged and contrasted. Also the orchestration has a strangely ethereal character, resulting largely from the very sensitive writing for the wind. The opening tutti contains the two main themes, the first calm and dignified, and the second, built on shorter phrases against a murmuring background. There is also a haunting cadential passage that does not return until near the end of the movement. In the exposition the second subject appears in the dominant, leading to a very impressive patch of dark chromatic colour; the passage that leads back to the recapitulation has an extraordinary sense of vastness, the piano playing arpeggios against a very rich harmonic background. The simple design of the movement is particularly effective between two such energetic and eventful neighbours.

The final rondo is, as usual, rich in ideas; the first of these is very similar to a gavotte from the ballet music in *Idomeneo* and it suggests at once that the speed should not be excessive. Before long a temporary glance at C minor is reminiscent of similar things in the first movement and, like other passages in the work, has a decided foretaste of Schubert. The piano is silent for some time and, after a very formal and emphatic cadence, enters with a new theme of a more brilliant character. Some lively passage work, prophetic of certain things in Beethoven's 'Waldstein' Sonata, leads eventually to the main theme of the first episode, which is more lyrical. The central episode, as in K.488, contains two contrasted ideas, one in A minor and the other in F. The latter is in some ways the most distinctive theme in the movement; its more sustained melodic line and the more deliberate harmonic movement that this implies are particularly impressive in their surroundings. In the melody itself, the seventh and eighth bars provide a beautifully timed escape from what might otherwise have been a conventional sequence (Ex. 41). The continuation is equally beautiful, and the music that follows is extraordinarily imaginative.

The rhythm of the first two bars of Ex. 41 becomes the basis of a contrapuntal dialogue between flute, first oboe and first bassoon over a pedal note, the piano playing arpeggios. Reference has already been made to Mozart's skill in bringing back the main theme in a rondo. This

Ex.41

is a particularly fine instance and there is another, hardly less impressive, at the end of the first episode. It is passages of this kind that give this movement its individual character, and bring it into line with the grandeur of the first two. Usually it is on the strength of his stormier and more sombre works that Mozart's foreshadowing Beethoven is stressed, but it can also be seen in the spacious serenity of such works as this concerto and the first movement of the String Quintet in C, K.515. For many years K.503 was neglected; now, viewed from a distance, it can be seen as a masterpiece.

THE 'CORONATION' CONCERTO, K.537 (1788)

The Concerto in D, K.537, was for many years one of the most popular of Mozart's piano concertos. Now it is often underrated. The title 'Coronation Concerto' is unfortunate; it suggests something monumental, which this work, despite its considerable size, certainly is not. After the fascinatingly elaborate texture of K.503, it may seem slight and sketchy, but even its severest critics will probably admit that it contains some very characteristic music. The opening of the tutti, though less light-footed, has something of the exhilarating atmosphere of the Overture to *Figaro* and, as Charles Rosen has pointed out,[1] there are two curious moments when a new idea is preceded by a few bars of unaccompanied melodic line. Mozart, with his inspired showmanship, was always quick to discover any new means of displaying his ideas to the best possible advantage. The tutti contains all the material of the movement except the first theme of the second group; this is reserved for the piano in the exposition, and has some attractive chromatic touches. Another part of the second group looks back to Ex. 7, from the Concerto for two pianos:

1   Charles Rosen, *The Classical Style* (London, 1971).

Ex.42

The development section is interesting and eventful. At first, as in the much earlier Piano Sonata in D, K.311, he concentrates on the last phrase of the exposition, treating it with much resourcefulness. Then the music becomes less thematic, and there are some very attractive modulations before the recapitulation is heralded very effectively by a *pianissimo* drum-roll. The recapitulation is interrupted by the recall of a very pleaant passage from the first tutti that has not been heard since; this is followed by a surprisingly dramatic passage leading to the cadenza. For this Mozart has left nothing, though in the old Breitkopf complete edition the cadenza written for K.451 was wrongly allotted to this work. The end of the movement is disappointingly perfunctory, as though the composer had lost interest.

The sketchiness of the solo part in the autograph of this work suggests that it was written in some haste, and the slow movement, for all its undeniable charm, leaves a rather tantalising impression, especially if compared with those of K.491 or K.595. The orchestral writing, especially for the woodwind, is less imaginative than usual and, as in the first movement, the concluding bars seem curiously lame. But there are other more attractive features. The central section, with its occasional three-bar phrases and its modulation from A to C, has a pleasant flow, and points the way to a similar passage in the slow movement of K.595. And, most important of all, the main theme, which is repeated many times, still retains a strangely haunting and memorable quality which to many music lovers may easily outweigh any technical considerations:

Ex.43

This was the first time that Mozart used the ABA form for the slow movement of a concerto since K.415. There the result, though beautifully polished and graceful, was somewhat monotonous; here the texture is less subtly woven but the ideas are more striking and stand out more vividly. Of the two movements it will always make the wider appeal.

The finale is in an unusual form commoner in Schubert's music than anywhere else; it is a rondo with two episodes of which the second is a recapitulation of the first. In some ways it could be called a more light-hearted relative of the finale of K.503. The main themes of the two movements have the same gavotte-like rhythm with phrases beginning halfway through the bar. Both contain much brilliant writing for the piano, but the later movement has nothing like the richness and variety of orchestral texture, or the underlying spaciousness of the finale of K.503. But it contains a wealth of pleasant ideas, some of them highly characteristic:

Ex.44

The first episode, as so often in a concerto rondo, opens with a transitional tune in the tonic which leads gradually to new material in the dominant. When all this is recapitulated the transitional tune, after a very striking modulation, starts in B flat and moves in a fascinatingly roundabout way through a number of keys to the tonic. The coda contains a charming dialogue for orchestra and piano built on the first phrase of the main theme. The whole Concerto has suffered to some extent from its position in the series; it does not aspire either to the grandeur of its predecessor or the subtlety of its successor. It is more of a showpiece than the other two but, taken on its own very considerable merits, it remains an extremely attractive and enjoyable work.

THE B FLAT CONCERTO (K.595)

A few months later Mozart showed a totally different side of his genius in the last three symphonies. He did not return to the piano concerto until early in 1791, the last year of his life. The Concerto in B flat,

K.595, is therefore contemporary with *Die Zauberflöte*, and is in a far more intimate style than K.537. The opening is unusual. The first four bars, preceded by a bar of accompaniment, suggest the opening of a song, but it is interrupted from time to time by a rhythmic figure which seems unconsciously to recall the march-like themes with which several of the earlier concertos opened:

Ex.45

Another phrase vividly recalls one of the themes of the finale of the 'Jupiter' Symphony. The tutti contains some very appealing lyrical passages, and, owing to the absence of trumpets and drums, the more vigorous passages are more light-footed than in the more monumental works. After bar forty-six the Bärenreiter miniature score, based on the new complete edition, has restored seven bars which are in the first edition but in no later ones.

Despite the great differences in spirit between K.537 and the present work, there are certain parallels between them. At this stage Mozart is less concerned than before with unusual points of structure, and in both movements the tutti and the exposition follow mainly similar courses, only the first theme of the second group being reserved for the soloist to play in the exposition. The themes themselves have similarities: that of K.537, though in the major, shows a strong tendency towards the minor; and that of K.595 is definitely in the minor. But the most striking part of the movement is the development section. Starting in the very remote key of B minor, it is dominated entirely by the main theme and Ex. 45. They chase each other through an astonishing number of keys, without the least suggestion of strain or breathlessness. The texture is intricate but lightly woven, as in chamber music; eventually the main theme gains the upper hand, and the recapitulation is introduced with Mozart's usual felicity. His cadenza is beautifully planned, using first two well-contrasted ideas from the second group, then Ex. 45 and finally the main theme. Shortly before this there is a return of the only passage in the tutti that was not included in the second group; it has a nostalgic touch of B flat minor that fits well with the mood of the whole movement. Eventually the final bars of the tutti provide a neat and delicate conclusion.

The slow movement is very similar in general plan to that of K.537 and it has the same unpretentious simplicity. But of the two movements this is certainly the subtler and the more sensitive. The melodic ideas are equally attractive, and the orchestral writing far more interesting. There is a touch of *Die Zauberflöte* in the quiet solemnity of the main theme, played first by the piano and repeated by the orchestra with very rich scoring:

Ex.46

The central section is very similar to that of the slow movement of K.537, the phraseology is identical at first, and it goes from B flat to G flat at the same stage at which it goes from A to C in the earlier movement. But here it is done more sensitively, coinciding with a rising leap of an octave in the melody, and the return to the main theme, which in K.537 is rather perfunctory, is here carried out with far more sense of occasion. In K.537, the repetition of the first section involves hardly any change, apart from a few details and a rather slight coda. But in K.595, there are alterations of various kinds, one of which raises an intriguing problem.

On its final appearance, the melody of the main theme is doubled at the lower octave by the first violin, reproducing in the second and third bars consecutive fifths with the left hand of the piano part, with curiously Pucciniesque results. But in the autograph Mozart crossed out the chords in the left hand and wrote the word 'basso', indicating that it was to be played an octave lower, thereby avoiding the consecutives. In addition to this there are some delightful extensions and modifications towards the end of the movement including one bar that recalls, possibly by accident, the second bar of the main theme of the first movement. The part played by the piano in the last few bars is particularly charming. The comparison between this movement and the Larghetto of K.537 is not intended for the disparagement of the earlier movement. Both are full of Mozartian charm, but the later movement has deeper qualities as well.

The finale, in 6/8 time, has obvious resemblances to those of K.450